I0537930

Spirals

Spirals

A Collection of Poetry & Prose
from Utah's Northern Edge

Willow Park Press

Spirals

A Collection of Poetry & Prose from Utah's Northern Edge

Copyright © 2019 Willow Park Press

All rights reserved. The contributor retains all rights to his/her work. No part of this publication may be reproduced, distributed, or transmitted in any form or by any means, including photocopying, recording, or other electronic or mechanical methods, without the prior written permission of the contributor, except in the case of brief quotations embodied in critical reviews and certain other noncommercial uses permitted by copyright law.

ISBN: 978-1-7332908-0-7

Cover design © Willow Park Press

Cover and interior design by E.B. Wheeler. Photo from composite, "Spiral Jetty from Rozel Point," courtesy of Soren Harward (CC-BY-SA 2.0).

Spirals is dedicated to all the creative people associated with the Brigham City Writers chapter of The League of Utah Writers. And also to the loved ones who support them.

Contents

INSPIRATION

E.B. Wheeler

THERE'S A KNOCK at the door.

That's where I'm stuck. My protagonist is standing over her boyfriend's corpse, the murder weapon in hand, and she hears a knock at the door.

It could be the police.

Nah, no good. If they knew about the murder they'd break down the door, and if not, why would they be there?

Her best friend? Real friends help you move bodies, right? That's a bit cliché. So is the knock on the door, though.

The cat hops up and sniffs my screen, then steps on the keyboard.

aweawvghcbb

"We used that line last time."

I drop the cat on the floor, hit backspace a dozen times, and lean my swivel chair way back. My hair and arms dangle over the edge as I spin and stare at the patterns on the textured ceiling. I spot a horse, a dancing couple, and a dolphin with a creepy mustache. No inspiration there.

My ever-patient husband took the kids out, giving me the whole day to myself.

"You *have* to have fun," he said. "Get some work done on your book."

Crap.

Three hours until they come home. So far, I haven't had fun or written a word. I cleaned the bathroom, even reorganized the toilet paper, soap, and feminine hygiene products under the counter. Then I overthrew a new civilization forming in the back of the fridge. It may once have been lasagna.

If I can just get past this scene, I'll call the day a success. I'm sure the story will pick up from there.

I lower my foot, dragging the chair to a stop, and notice the cobwebs over the curtains. Ugh. How long has it been since I've dusted anything around here? My new vacuum has an attachment for curtains. According to the kid who sold it to me, it has an attachment for everything.

The box of hoses and brushes is as big as I am. I sort through them until I find the one for removing cobwebs from curtains. It works so well, I use it in the other rooms too, even the ones without cobwebs.

Back to work. My cursor ticks a steady rhythm, mocking me. How hard can this be? Pick the worst thing that can happen to your character and make it happen. So, a meteorite crashes through the roof and kills her. The end. Nah, that's not the worst thing. It's too easy.

I spin my chair, this time in the opposite direction. Maybe that's not a dolphin up there. Maybe it's a porpoise.

The cat slinks up, purring and wrapping herself around the desk leg.

"Didn't someone feed you this morning? I'm pretty sure it was someone else's turn to feed you."

I sigh and swing to my feet. The cat bolts ahead, her sagging belly swaying back and forth as she runs.

"Maybe you could stand to miss a meal. It might be time to give you a bath or something too."

There's still food in her dish. She just wants me to shake it around a bit. Still purring like a clogged lawn mower, she rubs against me, leaving a trail of hairs clinging to my black sweats.

The vacuum has a pet attachment too.

I glance at the clock. Two hours until Greg gets home with the kids. I've got plenty of time to figure out that knock at the door.

"We're home!"

The kids stampede up the stairs.

I shut my laptop with a scowl at the blinking cursor and the last words on the page:

There was a knock at the door.

The kids dart around the disemboweled vacuum cleaner sprawling across the living room. My husband scratches his head and stares at the scattered parts.

"Did you get a lot done?" he asks.

"Oh, yeah, I did. Thanks."

His jaw's working. I know that look. He's trying to decide if he wants to ask. Before he can, the kids squeal and giggle, pointing at the shame-faced cat as she darts for a safer hiding place.

A door-to-door vacuum salesman. That has potential.

I whip the laptop back open, hunching behind it to muffle my words. "The vacuum's clogged."

THE FIERCE ELIXIR

Dede Mattix

PERHAPS MY CHILDREN deserved better than this,
my wet-dog launch from a rescue canoe,
an embarrassing spectacle with flotsam in its teeth
ushering them towards a less precarious adulthood
than my own. Heaven knows
it's taken decades to steady myself, after surviving
the gauntlet of my own childhood. Now these,
my beloved, tagalong brood,
grow like various wildflowers cast by a random hand.

And they are bruised, despite my heroic trying.

There have been nights I've driven spikes of memory
through my palms, seeking penance for the ways I
know I've failed them.
And days my heart, at a thought, will crack wide open
like a gull's egg fallen from a cliff to the rocks below,
a broken promise carried away on
saline tides of retribution.

But love has been my fierce elixir, the fire that burns
within my veins.

I'd have sold my soul thrice over just to know it would
burn bright enough

to purge ancestral demons,
outrun the wolves,
or call down manna to heal their souls.

I feel unseemly as I reach to chisel out their captive wings,
only to find they've already flown from their pedestals.
How could these, quarried up, have come from such as I?
They shimmer in the moonlight, luminesce in the sun.
Light flows from their faces, bathes the faces of their young,
who turn to me,
not cumbered by the woundings of our past,
        and call me Blessed.

BLUE SCRUBS

Keri Montgomery

THE WOMAN ALWAYS comes at lunch, her attitude cheeky and persistent. She likes to wear pink sneakers with her powder-blue medical scrubs, and her routine consists of relentless nagging regarding my sleeping, bathing, and hygiene habits. Then if I've taken my medicine. Sometimes I lie.

But today, she didn't show.

"Tell them to come inside," I groan to the 911 dispatcher, then let my cell phone fall to the carpet. Two paramedics, carrying heavy med bags and a tablet, announce themselves from the front door of my ground-level apartment. "I'm back here," I manage to say aloud, my voice cracking at the effort.

"Ma'am, tell us what's going on?" one of them asks. He's a young man in his twenties who looks shiny and fresh from graduating his program—*green* and not yet frayed around the edges.

"My stomach hurts. I think I'm dying."

"When did this pain start?" the other paramedic asks. This one, a woman in her thirties, doesn't look as green. She's wearing her hair back in a tight, no nonsense bun.

"It started a little while ago. I don't know how long." The words stick heavy against my lips. Parts of my body— my mind and breath—are slowing down, and I can feel the world turning sluggish and distant. Or puffy and sweaty. Or pale and scorched. I can't tell anymore. "Fix my stomach."

They busy themselves around me like bees, asking endless questions about where I am, and what I'm doing, and what year I think it is—needless things. But I need their attention. Like an addiction, I *need* it. So I give the answers I want them to have. Then vitals. Pokes. Prods. Tests. I've danced this routine before, at times craving it between sessions, though my partners vary—sometimes EMTs or paramedics or police—but I cringe whenever the officers are the first on my scene. They ask different questions than the medics, ones hiding suspicions and judgements. They pry. I'm convinced of it. I've learned to pick my words with care so the dispatcher won't send the officers before the others.

"Any allergies?" she asks me.

"No."

"Are you taking any medications?"

My world pauses. Our dance has begun. "Yes." I point to the table near the kitchen where numerous innocent orange plastic bottles sit tipped over and empty, their child-proof caps littering the linoleum floor where I tossed them aside.

"Are all of these your daily meds?" the greenie asks, scooping the empty bottles and opening a plastic bag to contain them. They obviously plan to take me to the hospital.

Good.

They should.

Transport is the second part of our dance.

"Yes," I say.

Greenie paramedic types on the tablet as he systematically stows the bottles one by one. I study his innocent, boyish face, and his concentration on each label as he downloads my private life into his computer. He must see it. I know I'm right. Greenie must see how special I am. How I'm different than the others he's seen today. I'm a gift.

But he doesn't look at me, only the labels and the screen, though I know he's listening. He must be. Listening to me talk. And breathe. And exist. And be . . . special. I'm the reason he's here. The reason for both of them to be in my apartment. I call and they come. They run to me.

The other paramedic skips to the next question. She knows her steps in the dance by heart. "The bottles are empty. Are you out of meds or . . .?" she asks, the question lingering in the air.

Thrill shoots through my chest and settles into my stomach. I've planted the suspicions in her head. Pieces are coming together, and the seriousness behind her eyes is betraying her thoughts. The Tight Bun has also noticed how special I am.

Good.

She should.

"I took them all at once," I whisper.

"All at once? How long ago?"

I smile—subtle, with a single raised eyebrow. "Don't worry, I made sure we have enough time to dance."

Her eyes narrow.

I mirror her expression, squinting at her face, thinking maybe she's been here before. It's hard to tell them apart sometimes, only their uniforms. Tight Bun paramedic has smudged mascara in the corners of her eyes, right next to the newly forming crow's feet. I wonder if she knows how much her job is aging her towards burnout—dealing with all the fires and alarms and stubbed toes and prank callers. Not like my call. My call matters. The others are just noise.

"We need to take you to the hospital," she says. "Okay?"

I nod. Of course, they do. Special cases need special attention.

"Are you sure those are all of the meds you took? What about over-the-counter stuff, vitamins, or things from the cupboard? Anything you can remember will help the doctors."

"I only take my meds. Betsy counts them out for me, but she wasn't here today. So I did it myself. I figure that if medicine is good, *all* the medicine at once must be really good. It'll make me better faster."

"Who's Betsy?"

"The woman who's here at lunch. She always wears blue scrubs." I turn my head away, growing tired of more needless questions and letting my expression reflect the sunken, pale, helpless demeanor that I know a patient displays in a medical crisis. I do everything but literally paint the look on my face. Betsy isn't important. She isn't special. They need to stop asking about her. This is my dance, not hers.

"Is she a home care nurse? What health care company does she work for?" she asks.

I scrunch my nose and stare at Greenie again. He's still busy, typing my information with his young, firm fingers.

"Sometimes I think she works for herself. Doesn't pay attention to me. Or she would've come today." I say the words for show. Really, I'm relieved at Betsy's absence.

"Okay," Tight Bun says. "We need to get you into the ambulance, alright? You need to be seen right away."

I nod, eyes closed in somberness for a moment, though I'm grinning on the inside.

Greenie leaves to fetch the gurney and bring it to my front step, and I watch him walk away through squinted eyelids. Tight Bun hovers around me, gathering equipment and talking to dispatch on her radio. Then she's kneeling at my feet, collecting the tangled cords of the vitals monitor just as I notice movement near the open door. I expect to see Greenie's handsome face reappear, coming back for me.

But I don't.

That's when I see *her*.

Betsy.

Standing in the threshold.

23

She's wearing her pink sneakers and blue scrubs as usual, but something is different. On her face is scowl—a tightness that narrows first on the bag of empty prescription bottles and then on me.

A burning sensation sinks deep into my body, Betsy's anger drilling inside my core as if she knows exactly what I've done. Because she does.

Greenie reaches the doorway, and Betsy sidesteps towards the table. I move my gaze from her to him. He's so innocent by comparison, so young, and strong, and caring. I'd rather focus on his movements then feel Betsy's wrath. She's ruining things. Why did she have to show up at all?

Tight Bun stands up, turning towards the door. "Med control says to take her to St. Vincent's instead of Community."

Greenie nods.

"Fine," Betsy says. "I'll be there."

No, I say in my head. *Don't come. Don't follow me.* But Betsy must not read my mind because she never does what she's told. Instead I must be direct, and I can't show my disdain in front of my dance partners. It'll change our routine.

"Can you walk to the gurney?" Tight Bun asks.

"I'll try," I say. "But I need help. I'm shaky."

Betsy doesn't bother to move. Her face is stern, unforgiving.

Greenie comes to my aide, and they each take one of my arms to help me from the soft chair. Tight Bun lifts with skill and I soak in the attention, but Greenie's side feels powerful, sending electric shocks through my skin with each touch. I can hardly bare such interactions, and it would consume me in seconds, *if* Betsy weren't ruining my fun with her monstrous gaze.

They place me on the gurney, lightly weighted with a white blanket and with seat belt straps to protect me. Around my legs, they load up a red bag and the vitals monitor and straighten the cardiac wires attached to my chest.

The bag of empty meds comes with me.

But Betsy lingers for a moment, glancing around the room. I hope she's left behind. Forever. Even with my back to her, I can feel Betsy's stare eating through the gurney and devouring right into my innocent skin.

We roll away.

Outside, the light is fresh and the breeze fills my soul with more euphoria then all the medication that could possibly be churning in my stomach and seeping into my bloodstream. The gurney squeaks as it adjusts in height, and I cherish every second of this moment—the time when I'm the center of it all.

They're loading me, like a wave I slide inside the ambulance. Greenie shifts to the front of the rig and Tight Bun stays in the back. She's quickly fiddling with things. I don't pay much attention to her, only to the open back doors which I'm facing, to which I'm staring at Betsy standing there. She's two feet from the edge, her hands clasped together and her pink sneakers no doubt burning holes into the pavement below.

"I know the truth," Betsy says.

The breath shrinks from me.

"Tell them."

"No," I say.

"What?" Tight Bun looks up. She glances from me to outside. "Sorry, do you need something? We'll be leaving in just a second. We need to hurry."

"No," I repeat.

"Okay." Tight Bun stands and shuts the back doors.

I've won. Betsy isn't coming. She's shut out. I replace my lost breath in relief.

Greenie's voice fills the air. "Dispatch, Ambulance 14 is en route to St. Vincent's."

The radio crackles in response. A voice answers, "Copy 14, 12:57."

There's motion. We're moving away again, heading down the street. *Freedom. Attention. Care and concern and everything I want and deserve and—*

"Tell them that you lied."

My heart plummets. I can hear her, but I don't want to look up, to take in her face and her scolding.

"Tell them they are wasting their time."

No. I am not a waste. I see her pink sneakers first then the blue legs. She is standing inside the rig, but her body doesn't sway as the machine takes the corners of the road. Betsy's stiff. Forces have no effect on her, and she is rigid and fixed. No matter how much I want to rip the lead wires from my skin and strangle her with them, they would do no good.

I am not a waste. Leave me alone! The words scream inside my head. She must hear them this time and do what she's told.

Betsy never glances at Tight Bun, who's adjusting my wires and taking additional vitals. My heart rate is racing not slowing, which must be puzzling. No, Betsy's iron-clad stare is on nothing but me. The dance has changed.

And I hate it.

I hate Betsy. Loath her.

"Tell them you lied so they can treat you," she says, her voice cold.

They are treating me—like the special person that I am. I'm a gift. I look away from her.

"One that needs more medication, not pills pumped from her stomach."

I don't need medicine.

Betsy leans over me, her face so near I can trace the bloodshot veins in her eyes. "If you took your pills as the doctor prescribed," she says, "then you wouldn't see me. Now, tell them that you lied. Tell them that the meds ended up in the sink disposal right before you called 911, right before you strategically tossed the empty bottles in plain sight, and right before you decided to dance today."

I scream.

In pain. In anger. In vengeance. Screeching in desperation at Betsy's face and flailing my arms at her neck as if I could strangle her, but my grasp catches open air. So, I flail more and rage against my seat belts, a raw and visceral heat surging through my body from the small toes to the tip of my head. Pure fury fills my vision and tunnels my mind until I can no longer see the ambulance, or Tight Bun as she scrambles at my side, or the latched back doors behind the powder blue scrubs.

"I said leave me alone!" I cry at nothing and at everything. "You don't dance with me!"

Tight Bun is talking fast but I don't comprehend her words, and Greenie's voice is lost into the radio.

"She's lying," Betsy announces to the open air. "She didn't swallow a handful of pills out of ignorance. But she wants to be the center of the universe. Only she's not."

I've had enough, and tear at my safety belts, the white blanket, and the wires stuck to my skin. I rip and claw my way free until I'm standing on the cold metal floor, the moving ambulance swaying me like a buoy in the water.

"You don't deserve to be here!" Betsy screams at me. "You don't deserve their attention."

"Go away!" My hands are shaking. "I call and they come. But I never ask for *you*, Betsy. Leave me alone!"

Betsy straightens up, her face turning somber. "I can't. You won't let me. You keep me around. I am your doing. I'm your creation."

Her words sting. Like a thousand wasps, they sting at my skin and my mind and my soul. They stab at me. The ambulance begins to slow down, but I don't counter balance the motion, instead I'm fighting to stop Betsy's rock-hard words from rooting into my core. Then we brake fast, and Greenie is swerving. As I fall backward, Tight Bun reaches out, but I hit the ambulance floor. Hard.

We're stopped. I'm flat on my back—helpless. Like a bug.

The radio is squawking.

Tight Bun is yelling orders at Greenie.

Greenie is fighting his way to the back over a tangle of radio cords.

I'm ... not moving. My limbs are cement. Still. Quiet.

No, not quiet. I realize I'm screaming again—raw and involuntary until the shriek chokes in my throat. I gasp. Betsy is sitting still on the gurney now, her hands in her lap, and her ankles casually crossing those pink sneakers. She's staring down with a pinpoint gaze at my face, and this time I know my skin is truly pale. Not painted on for show. I'm sick. No, I'm sickened. Of her. Of everything. "Leave me be," I whisper from the floor. "Please ... Betsy, leave me be."

"I've tried," she replies. "But you've kept me with you since childhood. Remember? I'm the one who checks on you. And makes sure you're taking care of yourself. I'm the one who cares when others don't bother. You need to tell the paramedic that you lied about the pills so she can treat you properly."

I look over at Tight Bun, who's pulling things from the cabinets and shifting to get down low near my head. Greenie is around too, but there is such a fast-moving blur over me now that I can't track the tangles of arms and legs in medic uniforms.

I'm trapped.

My nerves surge in panic, adrenaline taking over and pressurizing my insides.

So I move. Again, I rip and claw to break free.

"Stay down," Tight Bun says. "Let us help you."

But I don't care. I want out. The dance is rotten.

I fight away from them.

"Wait!" Greenie shouts.

But I don't even care about his handsome face anymore. I'm past Betsy, who's silent for once, and I'm at the back doors, struggling with the metal latch. Before I can pull the handle, the doors pop open in unison. Two officers are standing partially obstructed by the metal, their posture tight and ready to move.

That's it. The dance is over.

"Ma'am," one of them says, "we need you to get back on the gurney." The phrase sounds innocent, but I don't feel it.

"You need to do what's best," Betsy says from behind me. Her voice is calm but sharp. "Now sit down."

I stare out toward the road, and at the cars racing passed where we're parked on the shoulder. Their metal bodies whip by so fast and defiant that I feel the impulse to run with them. The cars are free, but my path is blocked. Red and blue light flashes across my face, the brightness blinding me. And the noise—the sirens—sting at my ears. No one is touching me, but their hands are outstretched. I can hear their voices asking me to sit, but the words don't cut through my fog. Only Betsy's do. *Her* words cut through me like a knife, and she's loud.

My mind spins.

"Sit down," Betsy repeats. "Remember, I will always take care of you."

Everything stops. *I will always take care of you.* The phrase pulls at me. Memories flood in, images of tall doctors and hospital curtains and powder blue scrubs and helplessness. Of officers standing near me, the same ones who brought me there. And I'm small. A child.

The air inside the ambulance feels thin. The cars blur in the background. I stand still, unable to move or run or fight anymore, just shiver and feel defeated. Betsy's right. She's always right. I inch back. As soon as I sit on the gurney, my hands rest on my lap and remain still—waiting. The others cover me with the blanket and seatbelt me in again. A heaviness washes through my chest and out to my limbs, my expression sinking low with the motion.

"Tell them," Betsy says.

I glance up at Tight Bun. "I lied." My voice is weak. "I didn't swallow any pills. I've haven't taken my meds in a long time."

"Oh," she says, her eyes studying my face. "We'll have someone talk to you about that at the hospital. Well, after the doctors see you."

I look down at the blanket and sigh—more like I breathe the weight of a thousand sighs all at once. I know she means I'll be getting a psych evaluation, no choice in it. But I nod. An eval wasn't a planned part of my dance. It wasn't the last time either, which is why I had to move cities to change dance partners. Betsy told me the move wasn't a good idea, but I didn't listen.

And she was right. She's *always* right.

The others busy themselves around me once again, only this time I'm stone cold. I don't pay attention to their actions anymore. No thrill or flutter of excitement fills my insides even though I'm still the center of all. This attention doesn't satisfy my addiction because the dance is dead. Instead, I'm staring at the powder blue scrubs near my feet.

Betsy is standing tall in the ambulance, hands interlocked, smiling at me. "See," she says, "I'll always take care of you. Now, do what I say, and things will be fine."

I nod. *Yes*, I reply in my mind. *You know best. I was wrong to wish you away. You protect me. You are a gift.*

Betsy laughs. "Of, course." Her face turns stern—powerful. "I'm the one who taught you to dance. Never do it again without my permission."

I nod, like a child. Helpless.

FLASH ANTS

Kathy Davidson

THE ANT'S ANTENNAE examined the chunks of brown sugar before the ants set their mouths on it. I expected them to pick it up and carry it to their nest. But they just stood there, not moving. Others joined them and soon the hunk dissolved. They must be eating it.

I checked my paper. So, the sticks and rocks were ignored. White sugar was carried away. The apple and the beetle were torn apart, slowly, and carried away, presumably eaten. I wondered what else I could test on the fire ants in my back yard. My mom thought I was collecting data for the fifth-grade science fair next year. I just wanted to get away from my sister while my best friend Brian was out of town. It was a happy coincidence I met the fire ants. Then they became an obsession. Summer could be a little boring.

A pinch on my finger sent me into a shaking fit. I stayed too long. I danced into the house and changed my clothes. The itches didn't go away for an hour. I didn't mind watching them. I just didn't like them biting me.

I couldn't leave them alone. I wandered through the house, looking for something else to give the little buggers. There must be something else I could test on the fire ants. Something small enough they could carry, and not edible. I wanted to see if they carried things with their mandibles or their front set of legs.

Flour? Just ignored. Cheerios, pulled with their mandibles. The fire ants struggled until the Cheerios broke apart. It was a long, drawn-out process, and the ants attacked me before I could watch them figure out how to get the giant rings home. They were all over, and I had to jump in the shower to get rid of them. I had little red dots all over my legs. Stupid ants, biting the one that feeds them.

My sister suggested the table. Imagine that. She helped me. I think she likes to have the TV to herself. I put up my mom's folding table and found out on the internet if I put baby powder on the legs, the ants couldn't climb up and get me. This was great. I could watch them for hours. I tried all kinds of insects and even the mouse my dad caught in the basement. He thought I was crazy for wanting it but gave it to me anyhow.

Then I found the gun powder. The grains were the right size, and maybe they wouldn't eat it right off and carry it away. I filled a shot-gun shell and carried it outside, careful not to let my dad see it.

The ants loved it. They grabbed the grains in their mandibles and rushed down into their tunnels. I wanted to see where they took it. Were they eating it? What would they want with gun powder? I didn't know, but I had to give them more. And then some more.

The bag of gun powder was soon empty. The ants still came for more.

Mom was tickled pink to see me outside doing something. She told me so. Whatever makes her happy. I couldn't wait for Brian to get home to see if this could make a great science fair project. If I only knew what the ants were doing with the gun powder.

Brian wasn't so sure about the ants until I showed him how they ate beetles. The table wasn't quite big enough for the both of us, so he brought his mom's craft table. He had to see the ants devour every kind of insect, and we found a dead bird by the side of the road. It took hours for the bird to be devoured down to its bones.

That's when I mentioned the gun powder. Brian found some more in his dad's shop, so we fed the ants that too.

It wasn't long before we decided we had to light the gun powder. Maybe it would blow a hole in the ground where their main nest was. Maybe it would light the backyard on fire. I felt bad for the ants, but Brian was so excited about it, I relented.

We didn't know how to start. The gun powder was underground. Brian decided on a fuse. I insisted we wait until night. The fuse went in one of the holes with a little work.

I jumped on my table and Brian lit it.

"Did we miss it?" Brian asked.

I thought I saw a few sparks, but nothing exciting. Maybe my fire ants survived. They could have eaten the gunpowder, or the grains were too far apart. Brian had to try again and stuck another fuse in the nest. It fizzled some but was still disappointing.

The next morning there was no movement. Not one ant anywhere. I dug a hole in the nest and there was nothing. A few eggs survived, but no one to care for them. It was a little sad. To cheer me up, Brian asked me over to his house to play video games.

The real damage didn't show up for a week. My dad brought me into the backyard and showed me the spider web of dead grass that covered five yards. He could tell by my expression that I had something to do with it.

My fire ants had carried the gunpowder through tunnels reaching five yards! The tunnel system was massive. I missed my fire ants, but the rest of the neighborhood was thankful to be rid of them. My dad threatened me with grounding if I ever tried anything like that again, and I was lucky only the grass had died and not the whole neighborhood blown sky high. I agreed.

I asked for ants for Christmas, for a science fair project. I hoped I'd get them, only not fire ants, but the regular black kind. And a little gun powder, just to see what they would do with it.

FRAG · MENT · ED

McKel Jensen

MY DREAMS OF the future are fragmented,
broken, dangling in participles
and missing punctuation in crucial parts.

I've got the nouns, articles,
some commas … but you left.
Taking my verbs.
My proper nouns.
All the good adverbs
and adjectives.

You left me: *fractured,*
lonely, mournful,
the lowercase of *hope,*
and a whole lot of question marks.

CALLED LOVE
Dede Mattix

LOVE IS A TERRIBLE opiate to give to a child.
We giftwrap it in our cellophane pleasantries,
serve it up chilled on company china.
We bid our children cough up their wills
into our threatening palms,
embezzling their egos in their very best interest.

Our smiles plot their torment,
our caresses conspire distress
while magical fingers clasp us closer in their hunger.
We afflict them with our eyes,
with our tongues scissor off great portions
of divine innocence. We trample their allegiance
leaving their marrow a thin bleeding wire.

Promethean babes, cabled to our benevolent cliffs,
have their entrails kindly sundered
as they beam their neediness through veils of tears.
Reaching desperately for that drug,
they swallow whole
the wretched failures of calming vultures
whose deadly bills croon cradlesongs at sunrise reenactment.
In what diverse and deliberate ways
we cannibalize our young.

THE HITCHER

Mike Nelson

TIRED AFTER ANOTHER long day's work, I flip on the ten-o-clock news just in time to catch the interview. Roger Bingham, a thirty-eight-year-old father of three, and his old light-green Ford pickup truck is still missing after a year. Bad as that might be, it gets worse for me when I know I could have probably prevented his disappearance.

Times were crazy busy at work on that terrible day. I had to sacrifice a day of my precious weekend to catch up. I didn't get paid for overtime, so the thirty-minute commute to Thiokol from my home in Brigham City just added to my aggravation.

My commute only covered a couple of miles of freeway before I had to exit onto west-bound Highway 13. The last real civilization, if you could call the tiny town of Corinne that, lay about six miles west of the freeway. From there, the road crossed a single set of railroad tracks and then pushed straight west past a dwindling series of farms. The last fifteen miles or so passed through mostly wetland and then desert.

My normal weekday start time was seven in the morning, but whereas I was more or less being forced to make a Saturday appearance, I decided a little passive rebellion was in order. I didn't leave my house until eight. I've often thought that if I'd left about six-thirty as usual, I wouldn't even be telling this story.

Everything was normal until I took the freeway exit. At that point, several things happened in rapid succession that would affect me the rest of my life.

The northbound exit joined the two-lane road just before it passed beneath an overpass. *He* was standing on the roadside, just under the bridge, dressed in a long tan business overcoat that hung open in the front, revealing a suit and tie beneath. A matching felt fedora business hat crowned his head. He gripped a briefcase in his left hand as he held out his right thumb to solicit a ride.

From afar, the man appeared to be someone from our management team who'd possibly had car trouble on the freeway, and perhaps needed to get out to the plant for a Saturday morning meeting. Why else would a man in a suit and tie be standing alongside the road, soliciting a ride west towards a sleepy little farm town? If I picked him up, and he *was* management, it might've helped advance my career.

Having only milliseconds to decide, I ignored my common sense, braked hard, and pulled over.

The first thing I noticed when he reached for the door handle was his scruffy beard. It appeared that he hadn't shaved in a few days. I thought that rather odd for someone all dressed up. Before I could react, the passenger door swung open, he slid inside, and closed the door behind him.

What happened next, I could probably best describe as *sensory overload*. He stunk! An almost nauseating mixture of stale tobacco smoke and harsh body odor instantly filled the somewhat shabby interior of my old blue Chevy Vega. The nearly shoulder-length hair protruding from under the back of his hat was so greasy that it appeared as if he hadn't washed it in days, or maybe weeks.

I had barely begun to recover from the blast of foul air when the *other* sensation flowed over me. I can probably best describe *that* sensation as what you might feel when you're watching a horror movie and the damsel in distress is going to be murdered in a most heinous manner. You know, the bad guy is hiding behind door number one, and the damsel is about to open *that* door! It was as if the devil himself had just seated himself beside me. I didn't dare look in his eyes for fear I'd see glowing red orbs.

I instantly began to sweat. I could barely breathe. I wanted to wrench my driver-side door open and roll out into traffic to get away from him. Death on the undercarriage of a speeding bus would have been a mercy killing by comparison to what I knew this guy was probably capable of doing to me.

Being too chicken to face certain death by bus, I asked in the calmest voice I could muster, "Where you headed?"

He looked right past me with dark featureless eyes, and then turned his head and peered west through the windshield before he answered. "Where does *this* road go?" he asked.

What few hopes I'd had that my emotions were playing tricks on me fled, and blind unreasonable fear filled my soul. This man certainly wasn't one of our executives, and he wasn't headed to the plant. He probably had no idea where he was or where he wanted to go. All he needed was a ride. Now he had one.

I threw caution to the wind and looked over at him. At first, he simply stared ahead. Then noticing my stare, he turned his head to look at me.

His eyes, if not totally black, were close to it. I could see my own reflection in his glossy pupils. A scene from the old movie *Jaws* raced through my mind. Quint, the skipper of The Orca, was talking about what it was like to look into a shark's eyes. With a sort of half smile, he described them as: "Lifeless eyes. Black eyes. Like a doll's eyes."

I didn't think it was possible, but when I saw the man's eyes, my terror only deepened. It was if I was looking into a dark, bottomless pit. He had no soul.

I didn't dare glance down at the briefcase he held on his lap, afraid if I looked at it, and it held a handgun or knife, he might rip it open and shove a weapon in my face. I was trapped like a rat in a cage.

"It goes west," I somehow managed to answer. "There's a small town about six miles from here. Then the road splits. One route goes north through Bear River City and Tremonton, and the other keeps going mostly west." I didn't tell him that there were literally hundreds of square miles of sage, rocks, and rolling hills beyond the plant where my body might never be found.

From the stony look on his face, I knew that wasn't anything he wanted to hear. Then I thought about my wife and kids. I'd heard somewhere that if you were ever car-jacked or abducted, you never wanted to go blindly where your attacker told you to go. The obvious problem was the options associated with resistance weren't the most pleasant to think about.

I suddenly knew what I needed to do. First, I needed to get up to highway speed so if he pulled a gun, I could yank the wheel, sending the car careening into the ditch. If I was going to die, I wasn't going to let him leave my body lying alongside a lonely stretch of road or bury me in a shallow grave somewhere. I at least wanted my family to be able to find my remains. With any kind of luck, maybe the crash would either kill or maim him. Dying wasn't part of my plan but if it came to that, I would rather have some choice as to how I met my end.

"I can take you as far as Corinne," I offered quickly as I looked over my left shoulder and accelerated hard into the light morning traffic. "I live there," I lied. "There's a small bar and grill in town where you can get something to eat if you're hungry."

I couldn't tell if he was thinking about opening the case he was clutching in both hands, or if he was just concerned that it might fall off his lap as the car accelerated. Then I noticed that he hadn't fastened his seat belt, and a slight glimmer of hope shed light on an otherwise dark, black situation. I was belted in, and my old car didn't have airbags. I would probably survive a violent crash if it came to that. He wouldn't.

I pushed my speed up to sixty-five—ten-over the limit—and started paying close attention to both sides of the road, and to what little on-coming traffic there was. I really didn't want to hit another car head on in my compact car, but even that was an option. The borrow pits alongside the road weren't very deep. *Ditch-diving* might not be very effective at that point because the car would probably still be drivable after we crashed, and after he murdered me.

Then in my mind's eye, I saw the Bear River. Not far out of Corinne, the road had been built up to cross a marshy area, eventually crossing the river bridge. If I had to 'ditch' the car, that stretch of road would be the perfect location. The steep shoulders would almost certainly result in a roll-over, leaving the car undrivable. The real problem was, whatever I did, I had to do it before I got to Corinne. I knew I couldn't take him any farther west.

I took a slow, deep breath, trying in vain to convince myself that I was jumping to conclusions. Maybe my emotions were just that—*my emotions*—stirred up perhaps by guilt over having picked up the stranger in the first place when I obviously knew better. I tried to send my thoughts to a happier place, but they refused to go. There was a dark, almost palpable, spiritual energy filling the car that I simply couldn't ignore.

Our lack of communication stood between us like a concrete wall. Maybe if I befriended him . . .

"You in a hurry?" he asked tensely, glancing briefly at me.

"Oh, sorry," I apologized as I eased up on the accelerator. "I work nights. I'm just anxious to get home and get some sack time."

Easing up on my speed was a good thing. If I made him nervous enough to fasten his seat belt, I'd have no advantage in a crash.

"Is there a motel in town?" he asked. "I've been on the road a while and I could use some rest."

"Sorry," I said. "There isn't. You'd need to go fifteen miles or so north to Tremonton, or about the same distance south to Ogden. I could take you back to the freeway if you want. You'd have a better chance of finding something in Ogden."

He looked out of his side window for a few long moments without answering.

I slowed even more, anticipating and mostly hoping that he'd agree to go back.

"No," he finally answered. "I could use something to eat and you need to get home. Just drop me off at the grill. I'll get something to eat and catch a ride back to the freeway later."

I didn't know why, but the way he'd said *home* set my teeth on edge. Maybe to him, *home* simply meant more hostages, or someplace to hole up for a few days.

Then it all fit, sort of. His case had to be full of money. Maybe he'd robbed a bank. Worse yet, maybe he'd ripped off a drug dealer and was on the run. That almost certainly meant he had a gun. He wasn't maintaining a very low profile, dressed up in a suit and tie on the freeway. He needed to be able to vanish for a while until he could overhaul his persona into something more suited to life on the road.

At that very moment he was probably thinking all he needed to do was gain access to my *imaginary* house, tie up me and my family, or murder us and then take his sweet time to change his appearance. He could eat, clean up, rest a little, and then drive away in my car. How less conspicuous would that be? And now it seemed, the lie I'd just told him was going to only further complicate things. I didn't know anyone in Corinne. I couldn't just pull up to a random house and play like I lived there.

"That suits me," I finally answered, as I accelerated back to highway speed. "Sorry I didn't ask where you wanted to go when I picked you up."

"No problem," he said mostly to himself.

I began mulling over a second option in my mind. Maybe I wouldn't have to risk dying in a car crash after all. Mim's Bar and Grill sat right next to the Bear River Valley Co-Op. Farmers were mostly early-risers, and the gas pumps right outside the glassed-in sales counter would probably be busy. I glanced quickly at my gas gauge. It read nearly full. I hoped he hadn't already noticed it. If he had, that would ruin my "needing gas" ruse. At any rate, I could point out the bar as I pulled off the road and drove past it to the Co-Op. If he called my bluff then, I seriously considered crashing my car into the side of the Co-Op, or into the gas pumps.

"You feeling okay?" the stranger asked. "You're sweating like a pig."

My heart sank. My mind, it seemed could come up with all manner of scenarios, and plans to thwart each, but my emotions were out of control. It certainly wasn't hot inside my car, and in fact, until just before I picked up the hitcher, I'd had my defroster running to dry up a little mist that had collected on the inside of the windshield in the cold morning air.

I didn't know how to explain my sweat. Then his stench came to my rescue. "I'm allergic to cigarette smoke," I nearly choked on my lied reply. "I know you aren't smoking, but I can smell it on you, and my body is over-reacting."

"Oh, sorry," he quickly replied as he rolled down the side window. "Will that help?"

I didn't know if the air circulation would dry up the sweat, but I hoped my lie would ring true in his ears. If he knew I was hanging by my fingernails on the very edge of self-control, he might make his move sooner rather than later. I needed him to remain calm and give me a couple more miles to work on my escape.

"That's better," I said. "Thanks."

He nodded but didn't say another word.

If only I knew what he was thinking, I raged inside. *He's too polite to be a crook. Maybe I'm all stirred up over nothing. Other than the obvious fact that he hasn't had a change of underwear or a shower in a while, he hasn't done anything aggressive—yet.*

Then other thoughts ran through my mind. It had been said that both Ted Bundy and Jeffrey Dahmer, in spite of being cold-blooded serial killers, had both been described as charismatic, even charming. Obviously being polite was no judge of a man's character, his intents, or what evil spirits he may have riding around with him.

Another thought fought for my attention. If it wasn't for that *other* sensory input still filling the car, I might want to talk to this guy. Talking might be good. It might relax us both. There had to be a story. Then suddenly I knew I didn't want to irrevocably become part of *his* story.

I firmly gripped the wheel. We had nearly reached the elevated roadbed. I could see the river bridge a quarter-mile ahead. It was decision time. If I was going to crash the car, I had to act soon. A long guard rail extended towards me alongside the road, curving outward on the leading edge to catch my car if it ran off the road so it wouldn't crash into the river. It was now or never! I tensed, gritted my teeth, and braced for impact.

Self-preservation, it seems, is strong. After all, he hadn't done anything—yet. I hesitated a few seconds too long. The end of the guardrail flew by, followed by the bridge deck, and then by another piece of guardrail. A few hundred yards ahead, I could see the reduced speed limit sign. Beyond that sign, there simply wasn't anyplace to ditch the car until we left town.

I tried to swallow, only to find the membranes in my throat dry and sticky. Saliva refused to flow. My hands began to tremble imperceptibly under the strain, and I had to release my grip on the wheel a little before he noticed. The forty-mile-per-hour speed limit sign flashed by, and I lifted my foot off the accelerator. I needed to be traveling at a reasonable speed in order to pull off the highway into the business' joint parking lots.

I silently prayed for people. Anyone would do. I needed an audience. Maybe a small throng of people standing around as witnesses would thwart any plans my passenger had, and give me time to get out of my car and run.

A couple of cars passed by going the other way, but the main road through town seemed otherwise deserted. I tried to keep my eyes on the road, but I left half an eye glued to the brown leather case straddling his thighs. If he was nervous, he didn't show it. His long, thin fingers gripped the front edge of the case but didn't move towards its latches. If he didn't have a weapon in the case, maybe he was wearing a shoulder holster under his suit jacket.

The Co-Op and the bar sat side-by-side just ahead. My heart sank. There was only one car parked in front of the bar, and none in front of the Co-Op. Then I noticed the red neon *open* sign in the bar's front window.

"That's the grill I was telling you about," I said, pointing at the building as I slowed down. "It looks like they're open."

There was no curb marking the departure point between the highway and the business' parking lots, so I pulled off the road, passed the bar, and aimed my car at the empty slot between the gas pumps and the Co-Op's front door.

"I need to stop for gas before I go home," I said as I braked to a stop alongside the pumps. Before he could react, I switched off the ignition so the gas gauge would drop to zero and pulled out my keys. "Sorry I can't take you any farther."

Not waiting for his answer, I wrenched my driver-side door open and nearly leapt out of the seat. Then I slammed the door behind me, perhaps a little too hard due to the raging adrenaline coursing through my veins. I hurried around the front of the car and pushed through the Co-Op's glass front doors.

A short, thin, mid-fifties woman with short-cropped graying hair looked up at me curiously from behind the sales counter.

"Something wrong, son?" she asked.

"I picked up a hitchhiker," I blurted out. "I think I'm in trouble."

A look of dread crossed her face as she glanced anxiously through the store's front windows and then moved along the counter a little so she could see my whole car.

"I don't see anybody," she said.

I whirled around, expecting the man to be standing near the front doors. There was nobody there. I stepped closer to the front windows so I could see the side of Mim's Bar and Grill. The parking lot was empty.

Is he lying down in the seat? I wondered. I moved to the front doors with caution and looked down on an empty passenger compartment.

I suddenly doubted my sanity.

"Do I need to call somebody?" the woman behind me asked.

"Did you see anyone walk away before I came in?"

"Sorry, hon, I was lookin' through the want ads. I didn't even know *you* was here until you walked through them front doors."

Without saying a word, I pushed one of the double doors open a few inches and searched the storefront and the side of the road. I then stepped outside and walked to the corner of the building, cautiously peering down the far west side. I half expected to find him relieving himself beneath the elevated fuel tanks. But no one was there.

The woman had walked outside with me. "Are you sure you're feelin' okay?" she asked. "You're all sweaty."

I suddenly didn't want to explain. She hadn't seen anyone else, therefore there simply was nobody but *me*. She probably thought she was dealing with a madman.

I hurried to climb back behind the wheel, started the car, and sped off. The stranger, if there had really been one, was gratefully gone. He was no longer my problem.

As I reached across the passenger seat to roll up the far window, a certain and familiar vile stench wafted up from the seat where the hitcher had been seated only a few moments before. Without that vivid reminder, I may have convinced myself that he'd been a figment of my imagination.

I turned left at the "Y" in the road. The single railroad track lay just ahead. Out of habit, I looked left and then right before I crossed the tracks. Then I saw him. He was walking towards Bear River City on the other road.

As I watched, he turned around, stopped, and held out his thumb. An old, light-green, 4x4 Ford pickup truck stopped alongside him. In horror, I watched as the stranger stepped inside the cab. I wanted to scream out a warning, but I knew the other driver couldn't hear me and it was too late. At that moment, the driver was probably already feeling what I had—dread.

I wanted to turn around and follow the truck, but what could I do? I wasn't armed. I didn't have a cell phone. All I could do was follow and serve as a material witness, if it came to that. But I suddenly didn't want to get involved again. I was free and emotionally shot. I took a deep cleansing breath, focused on the road ahead of me, and accelerated away.

I nearly threw up in my mouth later that night, as I watched the ten-o'clock news. A young local farmer was missing. They showed his picture, standing next to his wife and three children. In his picture, he wore an infectious smile—just the nice kind of guy who would stop to help a man down on his luck. Although they showed a picture of his missing pickup truck. I didn't even have to look at it. I knew exactly what I'd see.

I picked up the phone half a dozen times, but couldn't make the call. If I told the cops what had happened now, they'd brand me as a coward. Everyone would see my picture on the news. Then I wondered if the sales clerk at the Co-Op would call? If she did, they'd be looking for me as a material witness anyway.

Then I thought about what my own family would be going through if it was me who had gone missing. Coward or not, I had to make the call.

A deputy came to my door, and I stumbled through an explanation and a vague description. When I told him about the *entity* that had been riding along with us, his countenance dropped. It was obvious he understood what I was saying.

He asked a few more questions, scribbled a few notes on a wire-bound pad, then took my phone number and left.

As I glare at the TV screen, Roger's wife cries her way through the interview. My dreams are still haunted by memories of the hitcher's eyes. I could have done more. I should have done more! Guilt still torments my soul.

I silently wonder where that hollow-eyed spawn of Satan is today. Does he still walk the highways in search of another victim?

PATHS

Steve Odenthal

THE OLD MAN walked,
Stooped and somehow broken
With homage to age, the youth had spoken
Inquiring again of this ancient wonder
Which course was right, and which asunder.

'Tis not for me, the old man said
For I cannot change the path that I've tread
But look to your heart, let it be the guide
Make a choice from what lies deepest inside
Don't settle for less, as most of us do
Seek what you want, and then see it through.

But how can I choose, the youth fairly pleaded
I do know my heart, but in this world, is it needed?
The words are inside—they are mine, and so right
But is there such a place? Do I dare give them light?

The old man sat down
On a rock, heaved a sigh
Smile on his face and a glint in his eye.
His countenance changed as he looked to the sea
He spoke softly now to the youth at his knee.
What makes you believe that I know your way?
'Twas always safe passage brought me to this day

Spirals

I took the roads traveled by more than a few,
Never seeing the great wonders this world offers you.

The youth thought on this, then rose from his seat
Your guidance is good and I've learned at your feet.
Your thoughts have been mine and the opposite true
But decisions are made then right or wrong, seen through
I won't see you again if my dreams are fulfilled
I'll be doing my best, a lifetime to build.

You will be just fine, the old man thought.
The youth heard this and emotions he fought.
The two of them parted that day in the sun
Not really leaving, for, of course, they were one.

LIMBER LUMBER

Betti Avari

CAMPING IS USUALLY peaceful, but tonight the Rocky Mountain air carries a rumbling voice on the wind. "Limber Lumber!"

"Steve, wake up!" I tug on his sleeping bag, but it's no use. His sleeping pill has taken effect.

Outside the tent, I hear it again. Closer. "Limber Lumber!" It's followed by a rustle of branches.

With shaky hands, I reach for the flashlight. Should I turn it on? If an intruder knows I'm awake, the light could scare them away. Or, I fear, it could let them know right where I am.

Another rustle, much closer this time. I stop breathing.

To think I'm the one that kept telling Steve there was nothing out here, so far off the lumber trail. Nothing to be afraid of! And all the while, he kept joking that he'd never slept in a tent, but he'd spent many sleepless nights in a tent.

Now I'm the sleepless one.

It's pitch black, outside and in. No moonlight to cast shadows on the edge of the tent. "Steve!" I whisper. "Please!" Still nothing. I risk a few shallow breaths when I hear a rustle against the tent wall.

With shaky hands, I press the button on the flashlight. My pulse races, my throat constricts. "Who's there?" I yell out.

I sound too soft, too shaky. I need to sound fierce, so I try again. "Get out of here!" I growl. "You're outnumbered! I'm not alone!"

I hate bluffing, mostly because I suck at it—I lost more strip poker games to Steve in that dorm room back in college than I'll ever admit to our children someday. . . *if* we're lucky enough to live through this night and actually have children of our own.

Perhaps it's a raccoon or a badger? A sudden clicking, rustling sound echoes overhead, and I whip the flashlight toward the tent ceiling. The sound must be coming from the branches above our tent. "C'mon!" I yell, both to Steve and whatever is rustling in the trees. "Knock it off!"

Then my heart stops. There aren't any trees overhead.

We pitched our tent in the center of a wide meadow.

Thinking logically, I know that our tent is seven-feet tall, so the noise must be coming from a massive moose, or perhaps a bear.

And I'm Steve's only protection.

I hear the strain of the tent poles before I feel the pressure, but the warning sound doesn't buy me more than a second. The tent pole snaps and the roof collapses toward us. I jump toward Steve and roll the two of us off the cots and into our gear packs. I scream into Steve's shoulder and reach for the flashlight as it rolls beneath his cot.

Twisting to shine the light on our attacker, I look directly upward and catch a glimpse of a large face through the jagged hole in our tent. It's almost human but as big as a garbage can lid, textured and rough, black eyes leering at us. "Get away from our tent!" I cry.

"Limber Lumber," he growls with a smile.

I'm wondering if I've just met Bigfoot when his whole body disintegrates into sticks and flies at us . . .

"Tami?" Steve is finally awake, but I can tell he's still affected by the sleeping pill. He sits up and winces in the late morning sunlight pouring through the gaping hole in our tent.

"It's about time you wake up."

He catches sight of me and lurches back in alarm. "Tami, is that you?"

I'm still shaken from the night before and more than a little resentful that Steve wasn't awake to properly protect us. I grumble, "Who do you think it is?"

"What?" he asks, reaching for his glasses. "Who are you?"

"What do you mean, 'who am I?' The tent pole snapped and a crazy Bigf—"

"Limber—what? Why do you keep saying that? Where's Tami?" Concern twists his features.

"Can you not see or hear me properly? I'm talking Bigfoot! Your medicine—you need some coffee or something, 'cause I just spent the night scared for my life that some stick creature was going to come flying out of the woods at us again."

"Okay, okay!" Steve puts his hands up in defeat and backs out of the tent. "Just sit right here. Right. Here. I'll get you a forest ranger, okay?" He shakes the dust and sticks off of himself. "I'm just going to see if I can find Tami first." Steve is already running for the trailhead near the pine trees in the distance, and as I stand to join him, I hear a rustling of sticks.

"I AM Tami!" I exclaim and throw my hands in the air.

That's when I see it, covering my hands. A thick layer of bark. I reach up and touch my face. My entire body is covered in bark, just like the stick creature. Just like the Limber Lumber.

"Steve, help me!" I howl. "Oh, my gosh, help me! Help me!" Against the granite wall in the distance, the only sound is my echoing voice, "Limber Lumber! Limber Lumber!"

NIGHT LIFE

E.B. Wheeler

VAMPIRES ARE STUPID. And I don't just mean those sparkly Hollywood vampires. I mean the blood-sucking animated corpses that are only better than zombies because they hold their limbs together a little better. You're also more likely to run into vampires at nightclubs, though I once saw a zombie trying to twerk. Be glad you missed it.

Since the kind of drinks I serve at the club's bar don't interest vamps, I usually don't have much to do with them. But I guess every species has a subset of jerks who see a petite brunette and think, "Easy target."

So, I'm walking home after the club is closed. Everything else is closed too, metal bars pulled down over the doors of hole-in-the-wall restaurants and pawn shops, and the occasional streetlight flickering as I walk by. But the moon is almost full, lighting my way and filling the night with mad, beautiful energy. I grin and pick up my pace, my stiletto heels clicking on the pavement and my purse swinging from my arm.

Three guys push out of the shadows of an alley to follow me. They're way too quiet. Real people don't glide down the sidewalk like that, especially not in packs. They have no hunting technique though; they're bunched together.

As I walk, I twist my hair into a bun and stab a pencil through to hold it, then grab my pepper spray from my purse. I hate to draw attention to myself, but the threat is usually enough to scare off the creeps who get too friendly at work. I've never tried it on vampires, though.

A lone car whizzes past, and the guys drop back, but they stay on my tail. We take a couple of turns and emerge onto a residential street, all sedans and white picket fences. I slow just enough for the vampires to catch up, then I whirl and give them a sharp grin. Ugh, they stink. Corpse breath. They stop and stare at me. One of them glances at the others, and they all lunge forward at once. That makes it easier to hit all three with the pepper spray.

They shriek and cover their faces. Interesting. I suppose drinking blood keeps their juices flowing, and that means sensitive mucus membranes. While they're pawing at their faces, one of the guy's fingers fall off. Seriously, not even a healthy corpse.

I back away, ready to let bygones be bygones. But they're fighting through the pepper spray. They circle up on me, more cautious. I have to give them credit for persistence. And now they're acting like proper predators.

Time to get serious. I bend my knees and circle with them, feeling the rhythm of the hunter's dance, bracing myself for the attack. They flash sharp fangs, ready to feed. I can smell their excitement and the stale blood growing sluggish in their veins, even over the spice of the pepper spray lingering on their skin.

The one to my right lunges. I duck aside and grab his black trench coat, using his momentum to whirl him chest-first onto a picket fence post. All that's left are ashes.

The other two stare for a moment, perfectly silent. If they were smart, they would reconsider.

They attack.

Two on one is a bit more tricky. I drop to the ground and roll between them, ripping my nylons and skinning my knee as I come back up. They crash into each other, a tangled confusion of rotting limbs. I give them a shove, and one of them falls to the ground. I jam my stiletto heel into his heart, and he explodes in a cloud of dust.

The stiletto snaps off when it hits the ground.

"Now you owe me a new pair of shoes," I say to the last vampire. I'm limping on my broken heel, but the whole night is alive to me—every sound, every smell. My eyes sting from the remnants of the pepper spray, but I bare my teeth in a tight grin.

The vamp snarls and charges. I swing out of the way, but my heelless shoe throws me off balance, and the pain in my eyes slows my reaction just a heartbeat. He catches me by the throat. His fingers are surprisingly strong as they squeeze. I flail out, connect with his stomach. He doesn't even grunt. The night smells like blood—my blood, from my knee. Spots flash in my vision.

I let myself go limp. He leans closer, fangs bright in the moonlight.

I jab my thumb into his eye.

He jerks back with a yelp and paws his face. I gasp a breath and grab him by the hair, giving a twist. His neck snaps, but that's not enough to stop him. He shoves me, and I sprawl on the asphalt. Now my hands are bleeding too.

The vamp closes in, his head tilted at an awkward angle. I raise my hands. His pupils dilate, and he lunges for me.

I yank the pencil from my hair and hold it like a dagger. The impact jolts through me, and I have a moment to stare into the vamp's black, uncomprehending eyes before he crumbles to dust.

"Stupid."

I kick off both shoes and brush off my hands before picking up my purse. The near-perfect globe of the waxing moon shines as bright as dawn above me, and I smile at the warmth of its light. Even vampires should know better than to mess with a female werewolf, especially at certain times of the month.

ICE WORMS

Kathy Davidson

THE MEETING DIDN'T go well at all. Lars groaned at the thought of having to stay on this frozen chunk of ice another hour. He wanted to collect his bonus and take his shuttle to a warm planet with a beach. It would take a month to get this chill out of his bones. He wasn't told ahead that the thirty miners had families and wouldn't want to leave.

Why did The Company make the job so hard by not telling him the whole truth? Someone could have hinted that the foreman was a jerk, and no one listened to him. Lars figured it was his own fault for not looking at the history of the colony, but who would have guessed this group, unlike others, had become a generational colony in its sixty plus years.

Lars went to the shuttle view screen and called up the recording of the meeting to hunt for the true leader of the group. He'd missed the subtle gestures and looks that made it obvious the older woman in the back was the true leader—a matriarch. She turned to leave when the foreman stood to parrot his own words. Half the room followed her out. She was the one he had to convince to move. In the view of the exterior camera, a crowd was waiting for the tram to take them back down five hundred feet below the surface to their settlement. Lars heard there was a large cavern down there and it was actually warm. Well, not freezing.

He studied her face and ran the image through facial recognition. She was covered with wrinkles, and her gray hair poked out of her white parka hood. He didn't understand why anyone would put up with getting old when there were so many ways to fix it. He hated these backward planets, yet the more he looked at the chubby face covered with laugh lines that lit up even her eyes, he realized he could like this woman. The computer came up with a match: Agatha Griffin, married to Afton Griffin, the first foreman, coming to New Artic sixty years ago. She never worked for The Company, instead raised three children. One killed with their father; the other two left the dwarf planet at age. One grandson still lived on planet. She didn't pull a salary. Which was odd. How could she survive on an ice cube with no income? The Company sent supplies, but only to those who could pay for them.

The computer didn't identify the woman among the group waiting for the tram to return, yet she could have caught the first trip. Lars rewound the video until he found her walking through a doorway in the ice wall. *Could she be walking home?* Lars didn't think so. She waddled like her hips and knees hurt. Why didn't she get those taken care of?

He grabbed his Company issue parka and left the shuttle to follow her. There must've been an easier job than this—one planet side or he'd even go for a space station. Surely someone could use a professional negotiator.

The doorway opened to stairs going up. Lars groaned. He hated stairs. After about twenty steps, there was a corner where they continue to go up, probably to the surface. He looked longingly back at his shuttle. The only way to get off planet was to talk to Agatha. Groaning, he continued climbing. If she could make it, so could he. Lars stopped to catch his breath after several minutes and several turns. If he waited here, shouldn't she come down to find him? Lars slowed his breath and stretched his legs, climbing again. He couldn't take the chance she would find another way down.

The door at the top opened to blinding white snow that made the darkening shutters on his irises slam shut. It took him a minute to focus on the drifted snowy hills. The flat spacious vastness shocked him. It wasn't very often he stood on a planet's surface. He stepped back, almost tripping down the stairs. That was one way to get back down.

Where could she be? Lars eased out into the vastness and scanned the horizon around the shed. He found her looking up to the setting sun. Her white coat met the tops of her boots at her knees. Her mittens and hat were a striking blue, the color of ice with no air in it. They weren't

Company issue. She seemed to be talking to the sun, shaking her fist. Lars turned up his ear piece.

"You could've left me on a warmer planet at least. I don't know what to tell them," she said.

He watched her argue until she turned and nearly slipped off her feet when she saw him.

She chuckled. "What brings you to the sun deck?" Agatha stepped toward him.

"I was looking for you actually. I'm Lars Smith, the…"

"The Company Man," she interrupted him. "Come to move the miners to more productive ice balls. Yes, yes, I know who you are. As I'm sure you know exactly who I am."

"Yes, Mrs. Griffin, I came to ask for…" His feet slipped around on the ice.

"Oh, call me Agatha. I really don't know who Mrs. Griffin is, or was." Her ability to navigate on the icy surface was impressive.

She approached him and held out her arm for him to take as they walked together back to the stair shed. Lars was grateful for the contact. She was solid and her footing sure, where he almost fell twice.

"Walking on the ice is learned talent. You have to think of yourself as a penguin . . . little steps and lean forward slightly." She exaggerated the movement and waddled around in a little circle. "Have you ever seen a penguin?"

The little performance made him laugh. "Yes, once in a zoo on Earth."

She studied him for a minute, making him feel as if she was seeing the penguin through him. "When I was younger, I wanted to see one." She opened the door and stepped inside the shed. "Come on, our hundred-and-seventy-hour day is almost over. We'll freeze solid if we linger any longer."

Grateful to get in an enclosed space, he shut the door behind them. He started down the stairs, then stopped to look back when he realized she hadn't followed.

"Going up is easier than going down. I'll have to take the express." She motioned to a side door. "It's been years, but I've heard the slide is still a thrill."

Lars was curious. He climbed back up to watch her pull a square piece of orange plastic out of a cupboard. She carefully got to her knees and then rolled her ample rump on to the plastic.

"Do you think you can give me a push?" Agatha attempted to scooch forward towards the drop off. She was bigger than a standard size woman, but small enough to remain mobile. Lars figured his arms could reach around her middle and have his fingers touch on the other side. He didn't meet many people who chose to be that size.

"You're not really going to go down that way, are you?" Lars asked. He didn't want to aid in killing her off, although it might solve his problems. No, he didn't want to do that.

"I used to do it all the time. It's perfectly safe. This time of day it's the fastest. There's another board in the closet." Agatha looked up at him. "Unless you *want* to take the stairs."

Lars examined the plastic square he found in the closet. "This is prefab wallboard."

"Yes, it is." She continued to maneuver herself to the edge. "You know your materials." Agatha dropped off the edge and whooped as she gained speed and went around the first corner.

A lump formed in his throat at the thought of the ride. He'd never done anything like this before. The board was a rectangle about the length of his legs, with rolled up side and holes where his hands might grasp. He looked wistfully at the stairs. It would take a while to climb down, and he could hear the woman disappearing in the distance. He was losing his chance to convince her to leave this frozen wasteland.

The first drop took his stomach out and he dragged his arms on the walls, desperate to stop. He looked up the slide, there was no chance of climbing back up. Down was his only choice. He couldn't hear Agatha's woops so she probably made it. He sucked in a big breath and scooched until the next drop, gripping the board tighter and hoping for the best as he spiraled around descending into the center of the dwarf planet.

"You scream like a little girl." Agatha was sitting next to him when he came to a stop and opened his eyes. "I told you it was a thrill. Wanna do it again?"

Lars coughed, trying to breathe normally, then pulled himself to a sitting position. "It's a thrill. I'll go back up if you do."

"You're that determined," Agatha shook her head. "No thanks. I don't mind the ride down, it's the stairs going up I can't do again." She rolled over to her hands and knees, lifting her arm for him to help her stand. He scrambled to his feet and assisted her, only slipping once.

A thundering noise ripped through the air. The ground trembled, not enough to knock him off his feet, but enough to feel. Their eyes met and fire blazed inside her eyes.

Lars had to let go of her hand as she hurried over to another door panel. She palmed the control screen and swore when it denied her entrance.

She quickly took off her right mitten and the glove underneath. Lars thought she would try again, instead she slipped her glove under the corner of the panel and motioned for him to help pull. The panel cover popped off exposing the wires inside. Agatha went to work, deftly changing the connections.

Lars studied the vibrant, ice blue glove he was left holding. There was no marks or rips, the gold spirals that decorated the back wasn't even harmed by the sharp edges of the panel cover. He had never seen such fine work. He rubbed the silky fabric on his cheek, letting it send shivers down his spine.

The door slid open and Agatha waddled inside. He was wrong about this backwards outworlder—she had talents.

He stepped in the spacious office and screamed. His attempt to rescue Agatha, to drag her back out, only succeeded in landing him on his butt. He could hear her chuckle and ventured a longer look at the wall. The monster serpent swimming in the blue ice hadn't moved. As he studied it from this angle he could tell it was the work of a very talented artist. The details were impressive. The mouth revealed rings of sharp teeth and a thick tongue—no eyes were visible—instead tiny tentacles jetted out around its head and the body spiraled into the depth of the ice.

Agatha sat at the desk and opened a control panel to wake up the system.

"What's that?" Lars tried to stand, the spiraling creature throwing his equilibrium off.

"That's Harold. One of our ice worms." Agatha continued to work the key board, getting around the security system.

"Your ice worms? They live on this planet?" Lars held the back of a chair between him and Harold.

"Yes, but they're not that big. Most of them are smaller than your little finger."

This planet had a native species? No wonder The Company was trying to distance itself from the dwarf planet. If the ecologist found out, they would've had a hay day saving the planet. No doubt The Company would let it slip and leave the settlers to fend for themselves.

The com rang. "Agatha, what the hell are you doing in my office?" The so-called foreman, Chuck's picture, showed on the view screen.

"Your job." She didn't even turn to talk to him.

"We aren't staying. It doesn't matter if the chutes are opened or not," He said. The veins in Chucks forehead were about to burst.

"You might be leaving, but I'm not." Agatha's calm and decisive voice was impressive.

"Agatha, there's no future here." His voice was almost a whine. "We have to move on."

"I don't have much of a future, Chuck, but I do have a past and it's here. I'm staying."

Another face took the communicator from Chuck and started talking.

A thundering crack ripped through the ice interrupting him.

"Keith?" Agatha pushed the same buttons again and again. "I can't get the main gate open."

"Chuck told Simon not to worry about opening the chutes." Keith was holding Chuck at arm's length as he tried to talk.

"The gears won't work from here. You'll have to do it manually," Agatha said, nearly in tears. Lars put his hands on her shoulders, wishing he could help.

"I'm on my way." Keith's voice drowned out Chuck's constant tirade of how he was the foreman and he made the decisions and she had no right.

"Don't go alone. Take someone with you." She took a breath. "See if you can turn out the filters. The water will be too icy, and it doesn't matter if it's clean. The Company isn't coming for any more ice." She looked at Lars and he nodded in agreement. Keith yielded the com back to Chuck.

The room rumbled again.

"It's too late. They can't be opened." Chuck glowed with smugness.

"If my grandson dies, I'll feed you to the worms." Agatha rose out of her chair with the threat.

"If those meddlers die, it's not on me!" Chuck spat back. "I'm not the foreman here anymore. I'm being transferred."

His attitude made Lars feel sick.

"That's right. And you better get up here. The Company man wants to leave before the freeze." Agatha slammed her hand down and the screen plinked off.

She groaned and sank back in the chair. "He better live."

"What does he have to do to open the chutes?" Lars slid into the chair next to her.

"He has to climb down the chute and crank the gates open. He will get wet and cold. If he gets too cold, he won't make it home. Hopefully those who went with him are strong enough to pull him out." She pushed the frost off the arm rest, glancing at the screen. "All we can do now is wait."

Lars took a moment to focus on the room around him. Murals of country scenes were background to a monitor showing the tram occupants coming to the shuttle bay and blinking displays of the temperature on the surface, in the shuttle bay, on the ground, and in the ice. The numbers dropping every blink. He looked everywhere but at the serpent forever spiraling toward them but never arriving.

"How long until the shuttle bay doors freeze shut?" Lars poked at the plummeting temperature display of the surface. He'd never escape.

Agatha lifted her head. "You'll have about an hour. Then it will be about seven days until it melts enough to open again."

Lars shifted in his seat, hoping his shuttle was safe where it was parked.

Agatha flipped a switch and the view screen brightened to show the tram. Chuck and a few others were on board and had luggage.

It was hard to tell who they were with their parka hoods pulled tight around their faces. Lars didn't even get a chance to count their number before the view switched again. It showed a tunnel through the ice with cables running down the walls.

"Look at that." Agatha ran her finger down a line on the screen. "That's a crack in the ice. I wish I could see the other side of the tunnel. I hope it doesn't go all the way through." Just then three figures ran past the camera. "Be careful Keith." Agatha whispered to their backs.

She flipped the view to another camera, but the screen was blank, and a message popped up: *NO INPUT. CHECK SOURCE.*

Agatha took a deep breath and slumped back down in the chair. "There's nothing to do now but wait."

Lars studied the monitor when Agatha changed the view for him. "How long does the tram take to get to the top?"

"Fifteen minutes. We should know by then if Keith is successful." She toggled a switch to shut the door allowing the room to warm up.

Lars shifted in his chair. It protested and felt like the chair was going to give under his weight. Obviously, Chuck didn't want anyone else to be comfortable in his office. Agatha fingered the knobs and silently let the tears drip off her chin.

Lars' muscles twitched in the silence. "What will happen if the chutes aren't opened?"

"If the ice chambers aren't filled, then the weight of the ice above will crush them, leaving the walls of our cavern unstable." Agatha didn't move other than to answer.

"Would that be so bad?" Lars looked at the pictures on the walls. "The Company won't allow you to sell ice to anyone else."

"Oh, we don't care about selling the ice, but their collapse may damage our cavern."

The place they lived. "I'm sorry. I don't have time to see it for myself."

Agatha pointed to the pictures on the walls. "There it is."

Lars looked closer at the murals of grassy valleys with rock houses scattered around. "Are those goats?"

Agatha looked up. "Yes, we have goats."

Lars looked closer. "This is here? In the cavern? I wouldn't want to leave either."

"We have chickens too." Agatha almost smiled.

"Chickens? Like for real eggs?"

Agatha nodded.

"I wish I could stay longer." He put his fingers on the picture and realized it wasn't paint on the wall, but a fabric—a tapestry. "Where did you get this?"

She swiveled her chair and leaned forward to look. "I made it for my husband. I'm surprised Chuck didn't rip it down."

"You made this? Out of what? How did you get those vibrant colors?" It felt almost as silky as her gloves.

"Oh," she laughed. "It is one of the secrets of the planet and a curse too it seems."

Lars raised his eyebrows, hoping she would continue.

"You already met Harold, our secret." She ran her eyes over the consuls and the red lights blinked back at her. "There are billions like Harold all over the planet. The ice worms excrete the fibers that clog filters, making the ice unusable, and providing fibers to weave."

"I thought it was the sediment from the exposed mountains that made the ice unusable." Lars couldn't stop fingering the silky fabric.

"Oh, it is, in a way. The sediment is rich with nutrients the ice worms thrive on and with more mountains closer to the surface ice, the ice worms are able to multiply." She grinned like a proud mama. "Their silk thread is strong and takes dyes to make these beautiful tapestries."

"I don't know if The Company wants to buy anything like this."

"No, they don't. We've been selling it to transport pilots and a few visitors. It isn't much, but we don't need much." Agatha pulled off her other glove. It was skin tight and except for its blue color, it was hard to tell she had it on.

"The Company wouldn't allow that either." Lars didn't want to ruin their life, but The Company was the law in this end of the galaxy.

"When my husband negotiated the contract to come here, he made it possible for me to sell a few small things. We can only sell manufactured goods like gloves, coats, blankets, and tapestries. Not raw goods like ice and the fibers." Her hands rubbed her thighs in a nervous gesture.

"Really, I've never seen a contract like that."

"My husband loved me and wanted me to come with him, so he let me bring goats and my loom so I could weave. We never dreamed there would be anything so fine as the silk from the ice worms." Her smile didn't crease her eyes. She frowned at the ground. "This world has taken everything from me, but it's still my home and I intend on my bones resting in this ice next to my husband."

Lars somehow understood even though he didn't have a place to call home. His mother lived on transport running between worlds. Jealousy for a planet, especially a frozen one felt strange.

The ice rumbled and clanked, different than the other times and went on for minutes. When it finally stopped, Lars looked down at Agatha. She had her hands over her face and she was openly sobbing.

"What just happened?"

"The chute is opened and the ice tanks are filled." Agatha straightened her back and swiveled around to look at the consol. Most of the lights were green now, leaving only a few still blinking red. "It's done."

Lars let out a breath. "Can you tell if Keith is okay?" He leaned closer.

Agatha turned the monitor to the tunnel again. They held their breath and waited.

Several minutes past with only the wires and the crack running past the camera in the tunnel.

They both jumped when the heard Chuck pounding on the door. "Let me in."

Lars and Agatha just turned back to the monitor and let the ex-foreman beat on the door.

Agatha saw it first. Her breath caught as the lights flickered and shadows came into view. There were three figures, the middle one being carried.

Agatha cried out.

"He made it." Lars wrapped his arms around her.

"I hope so. At least they got his body out of the ice." Agatha took a deep breath. "I have to go down to meet them. Keith will need medical attention."

Lars understood her hesitation. "We have to open the door." The desire to stay burned in his heart, but he would have to deal with Chuck and the others who wanted to leave for better jobs. "I guess this is my cue to leave."

"Thank you." Agatha gathered her gloves and mittens. "See this spiral?" She traced the gold embroidery on the back of the glove.

"It's an ice worm, isn't it?" Lars wanted to touch the creamy fabric again.

"It's similar to them. They kind of look like cork screws, but this is my initials. My signature. See the lowercase 'a' inside the uppercase 'G'? It was my husband's too—our brand." She smiled up at him.

Now that Lars could see the swirl of both letters, he could tell Harold's spiral mimicked the brand. "I've seen the design before." He thought a moment. "My supervisor has a rope with that on his pocket." He laughed out loud. "You'll be fine here. Can I come back and visit sometime?"

Agatha stood to wrap her arms around him. "I would be disappointed if you didn't, but don't wait too long. I don't plan on sticking around too much longer."

The pounding had resumed.

Then she handed Lars the gloves. Before he could take the present, she pulled them back. "On one condition."

"Anything." Lars meant it too.

"Make sure Chuck gets so far away from here that he can never come back."

"You got it," Lars said. He took the gloves and brushed them against his cheek, enjoying the silk touch and sighed loudly.

Agatha's eyes sparkled until she turned serious and reached for the button that would open the door. Lars strode to the door, ready to race out and take the men with him.

"Goodbye, Harold. See you soon." Then he nodded for Agatha to push the button.

SEASIDE

Alice M. Batzel

LONG GONE ARE my youthful days,
the mirror so often shows me.
But joy and new strength I find,
through the gift of memory,
which brings alive my childhood,
when I lived by the side of the sea.

Now in my silver years,
my walk upon the beach
is not an easy stroll.
With stooped shoulders,
I carefully place my footprints.
It was not always so; I smile as I recall.
Once again, I stand tall, walk sprightly and strong.

Seagulls hover in flight and sing a welcome to me.
Rhythmic waves gently lap the sandy shore.
Smiling dolphins chatter in a call to one another.
Warm sand searches between my toes.
I skip and jump with my face pointing skyward.

Along the water's edge, I spy ocean treasures:
a furry sand dollar and a seashell or two beckon me
to lift them for a closer look.
A newly hatched sea turtle scampers toward the ocean,

and a quick-stepping miniature crab hides under its shell
as if to escape my peering curiosity.

I wade into shallow waters of aqua and emerald green.
Soft currents swirl around my feet
and tiny colorful fish tickle my ankles.
Deep blue waves invite me to come out farther,
and in response, I dive beneath their growing swells,
then victoriously ride the white foam back to shore.

A breeze slides across the water and over my skin,
drying the spray of salty ocean newly bathed upon me.
White sand scattered all about glistens like diamonds.
Sea oats reaching upward from the dunes
sway back and forth
in response to a rush of wind
inviting them to dance.

A greeting so grand as ever could be,
a more magical place there surely never was,
nor ever will be.
All cares and troubles which I might have
disappear from every sense
as I revisit my childhood
when I lived by the side of the sea.

WHAT WOULD YOU WISH FOR?

Rachael Jessop

EVERY SUMMER, my brothers and I got the chance to go visit Grandma at her beach house.

Grandma always said, "The beach house is a magical place. It's a place where wishes come true."

I'm a wisher, just like Grandma. I took every opportunity I could to wish big. Grandma and I liked to sit on the back porch and look up at the star-filled night sky, finding shooting stars to wish on. In town, at the wishing well, Grandma would give us a quarter to throw in and tell us that if we didn't wish big enough, it wouldn't come true. She liked to send us out on the beach, looking for hidden treasures—buried treasure of gold and silver, bones, and genie's lamps.

I loved the view of the ocean waves, the sunsets, and the people walking by. The smell and taste of the salty air and the feel of the breezes ensured that every year, everything we did was going to be enjoyable. My favorite part was playing with Grandma's new kittens. I was the luckiest of all the grandchildren. This year, I got to be at the beach house for my eleventh birthday. Birthday candles were always my favorite to make a wish on.

We had just arrived that afternoon. Dinner was finished and the smells of grilled chicken and vegetables still lingered in the air. It was my brother's turn to help clean up the dishes, so I went out onto the back porch to play with the kittens.

After a while, I decided to take a walk along the beach. I looked out at the familiar view that brought back so many wonderful memories. Somehow, I could tell that this year was going to be different. As the sun neared the far edge of the ocean water's horizon, a breeze of air kissed the back of my neck. Colors were just starting to form in the sky, and the air smelled and tasted sweeter than I had ever remembered it to be.

The winds changed direction. I didn't remember them blowing directly at me during this time of day before. In the distance, a whale jumped out of the water, catching my attention as it left a big splash in its place. That's when I saw it.

Something in the water reflected the sun's rays. I squinted to see if I could make out the object and to shield myself from the glare.

"What is that?" I asked out loud. I turned and scanned the area around me. There were only a few people walking along the beach that evening, and no one was acknowledging that they heard what I said. A wisp of air escaped my mouth as my hand brushed across my forehead. How embarrassing it would be to be caught talking to myself in public.

The item tossed up and down through the water. From a distance, the sides looked shinny and smooth. Probably from having water rubbed up against them for a very long time. As it rolled in the waves, I watched it push slowly closer to the shore. It appeared to have something sticking out of the side, which made it wobble in a curved direction while the bigger waves bumped it. I dragged my feet lightly through the pebbly sand as I walked closer. As the thing neared the shore, the sunlight stopped glaring of the object. Water rolled up to my feet and the waves reach the shore. I was nervous but felt comfortable by the familiar caress of the wave that cooled the soles of my feet before pulling away, receding back to where it came from. I let out a sigh of relief knowing the water washed the sand from off my feet. Oh, how good it felt to have that grainy sand washed out from between my toes. I loved the sights at the beach, but I hated the feel of sand on my skin.

A wave pushed the bright colored item up onto the sand and wedged it against a rock. I cautiously walked around the item in a circle before I stopped to take a closer look. Bending down, I narrowed my eyes to see if it was safe to pick up. After all, I didn't want to pick up something dangerous like a landmine. Lifting it up by its handle, I could tell it wasn't very heavy. Moving it from one hand into the other hand allowed some water to escape the spout and drizzle down my arm.

Upon looking closer, I saw that there was bright shiny red paint coating the outside, as shinny as the exterior of a brand new car. My hands moved across some embossed squiggly lines on the side. The shape of the item looked just like the genie's lamp I'd seen in the movie *Aladdin*. On one side, there was a picture of a faded white skull, and the other side had a picture of a treasure chest full of gold and jewels. I switched the item back and forth between my hands as I brushed off the sand.

"I wonder if there is a genie in this lamp?" I say out loud, half joking. *Life would be so much easier if I could just wish for what I want.* I was hoping for three wishes.

I started to day-dream about what I would wish for. As images came up in my mind, I begin to see smoke coming out of the lamp's spout. The smoke was light gray in color, weaving up from the lamp, but instead of dissipating like the smoke from a birthday candle, it kept coming and growing thicker. I coughed, waving my hand back and forth to escape the smoke. The smoke was lighter around the edges and came together in a dark thick center. That's when I saw a figure forming.

A genie! In my mind, he should be blue. *No, that's too much like Aladdin,* I told myself. *He's green! No, leprechauns are green. Red? Nah. Purple? Okay, that seems good. Purple.* I nodded.

"For my first wish, I want a new house," I blurted out at the purple genie.

Looking down at me, the brow on the genie wrinkled and he leaned in closer to me. He towered over me. He must have been eight feet tall! My head started to shrink down into my shoulders as I looked glanced at my feet. *What have I gotten myself into now?*

The genie was the tallest person I had ever seen in my entire life. And his muscles on top of more muscles made him look even bigger. He looked like he could lift an elephant. When the breeze blew in my direction, he smelled like men's cologne with a hint of fish. There was sharpness to his eye, yet in the very back of them, I could see a twinkle of light. He had no hair on top of his head. And he was wearing dark purple pants to match his purple skin and bare toes. Though he was very intimidating, his long curly mustache made me smile.

"*Je suis le génie de cette lampe.*"

My head jolted back. "Huh?" I said.

"*Soy el genio de la lampara,*" the genie said.

I shook my head from side to side. "What?"

The genie put his hand up to his mouth and then cleared his throat.

"I am the genie of this lamp."

"Oh," I said, my mouth wide open while nodding my head up and down in agreement. "I get it."

"I am the genie of this lamp," the genie said again, this time much louder. His voice shook me, and I stumbled back.

I started to speak, but he interrupted.

"Let me do my part before you ask for your wish," he said.

I swallowed hard. "Sorry." I managed to squeak out, like a child who had just been caught trying to steal a cookie from the cookie jar, right behind mama's back.

"I am the genie of this lamp. I can grant you three wishes of your heart's desire."

I stared at his face. Once he nodded, and lowered his hand, palm out towards me, I decided this was the signal that it was now safe to speak.

"I wish for a great big house where all the bedrooms have their own bathrooms, so no one has to share. There must be a video game room, movie theatre, and a giant toy room." I needed to give details so he got this right.

"Outside there needs to be a swimming pool and a hot tub. A big area of grass to run around on with a huge playground." I caught my breath. "And a trampoline too." I could feel beads of sweat forming on my forehead. My heart pounded in my chest. I took a deep breath and the next set of words rushed out.

"Of course, there would need to be maids to do the cleaning and a chef to do the cooking." The last little bit of the air in my lungs came out in a pathetic wisp.

The genie nodded his head and said, "*comme vous le souhaitez.* I mean, as you wish."

Poof! My eyes widened. There it was, even bigger and better than what I had imagined in the first place.

"My second wish is to have $500 billion dollars," I exclaimed excitedly while rubbing my hands together.

I thought about everything I would buy. I would buy new clothes, new cars for Mom and Dad, new furniture for everyone's rooms, a pet zebra, and new toys for the toy room. All the video game supplies anyone could ever want. There wouldn't be any more fighting over who gets what. I would buy a humongous box full of water toys to use in the swimming pool, and toys for the playground. I would buy a never-ending supply of my favorite foods and drinks. Grandma could have a new beach house built too.

Of course, I'd pay off any bills that Mom, Dad, and Grandma had, so they wouldn't owe anyone any money. I guessed I could even give some to charity too, just to be nice. That's what people say, when they win money, right?

The genie nodded his head and said, "As you wish."

Poof! There it was. A dump truck could have driven through my eyes at this point as I stared at rows and rows of duffle bags full of $100 bills—too many bags for me to count at just a glance. I started to jump up and down hollering, as if my team had just won the national championship.

"What is your third and final wish?" The genie asked.

I put my hand up to my face and tapped my fingers on the side of my cheek. I thought for a moment then I answered.

"Finally," I said, "for my third wish I want to own a giant farm, with friends to help me take care of everything." My family loved animals, so owning a farm sounded like fun.

I thought about the chickens, cows, ducks, sheep, goats, pheasants, peacocks, horses, zebras, giraffes, and other animals I would have on the farm.

"It will need lots of grazing area for the animals and all the supplies to be able to care for them. There would be a bird aviary for all the beautiful birds. But best of all, there would be a huge garden where I could grow all kinds of vegetables and an orchard with fruit trees," I said.

The genie nodded his head and said, "As you—"

Something wasn't right. At that moment I realized the water was up to my knees. *The tide has come in!* The water crept higher and higher up onto my pants with each wave. I could see stars starting to peek out into the darkened sky. A breeze whistled past me, and goose bumps started to appear on my skin. *I don't care if I'm wet.*

I fell out of my daydream. But my whole body felt the excitement of just thinking about what I would wish for from the genie in the lamp that I was *still* holding. After getting back to dry beach, I brushed the sand off the lamp with my hand. At this point, I was more concerned about what was in the lamp than the annoying grit of the sand on my hands.

Rubbing the lamp didn't do anything.

So, I tried different techniques. Still nothing.

Finally, my hand moved in a circular motion along the side of the lamp. The temperature of the lamp started to get warmer with my speed. Something began to move from within the lamp. Several little puffs of smoke came out from the spout. I smiled. I took a deep breath in as my chest, shoulders, and eyebrows rise upward. *Could I have really found a genie's lamp?*

"My life is going to be perfect," I said, squealing.

Bang!

Out popped a black and silver colored flag. On it was a picture of a gun and on the side of the gun was written: *Fooled Ya!*

I couldn't hold back my disappointment. I hurled the lamp, watching it sail through the air and land back in the ocean with a big splash. "Rotten lamp," I mumbled.

As I walk away, the weight of the water in my pants made each step heavy. The brightness of the sky started to fade away to darkness. The weight of my shoulders was pulling me down towards the ground. I kicked at the sand and headed away from the water.

Almost back to Grandma's beach house, I stepped down on the sand and my foot hit something with a hard smack. "Ouch!" I said, tripping and my body lunging forward. I crashed down onto my knees with my hands in front of me. Sand flew up into the air. The blood in my foot rushed into my toes. I turned myself over and plopped my bottom onto the ground. Not only did I have that bleak, gritty sand all over my feet and hands, I now had sand stuck all over my wet pants. I brushed my hands together to knock most of it off, then I touched my head. *Yuck, sand in my hair!* The sand had splashed everywhere when I tripped. *Nothing is worse than sand in your hair.*

After rubbing my foot for a moment, I carefully stood up and dusted myself off. I started to kick at the hard object that I had tripped me. Then I saw it—a lamp.

It was plain and a little rusty with nothing fancy in its appearance, nothing like the kitschy garbage lamp I found earlier. After seeing the details of the last lamp, this lamp didn't seem to be anything special. Even had areas with chipped paint on it. "I think I've had enough of daydreaming for one night," I said. I kicked it out of the way.

As I continued to approach the little beach house, I heard my grandma's kittens meowing. A smile came over my face. Four kittens ran over to greet me at the first step. I gently slid them aside with my feet so I could finish climbing up the stairs. I stepped over the kittens as they tried to rub against my legs. The sound of a stray *meow* from the corner of the deck drew my attention to a fifth kitten. She slowly stretches out then jumped down from the chair and came over to join the rest of us by the back door. I bent down to pet them.

The boards on the back deck squeaked with the shifting of my body weight as I petted the kittens and talked to them. The back porch light flickered and acted like it was going to go off any second. Using all of my strength, I leaned into the door to pull it open. *We really need to find someone to fix this door for Grandma.*

As I walked into the house, I called the kittens to follow me. Four kittens hurried in through the doorway. I called to the fifth and she arched her back and stretched out long, then with the wave of her tail turned and walked away in the other direction.

"Silly Cat." *Most headstrong cat I've ever met.*

I made my way into the house without her. As I closed the back door, I decide to leave it cracked just a tiny bit so the kitten could come in when she was ready.

This kitten, however, caught my fascination as I imagined what she could be looking at. Her ears perked up and her eyes started to narrow in on something on the side of the chair. Creeping along the ground, she made her way over to the chair then pounced at a light spot. A moth took flight and flew away from the chair. It danced around in the rays of light from the porch light and then went out over the sandy area below the deck. The kitten jumped up and down after the moth. In pursuit, the little kitten's legs got going too fast and she fell head over heels down the stairs and plop, sand went flying up into the air.

Down in the sand, she hopped around chasing the moth. *Clonk*, the kitten bumped into something hard. *Oh, poor kitty*. Shaking her head, she looked down cross-eyed at a lamp. She nudged her nose up and down while sniffing at the lamp I had tripped on earlier. Sand fell away from the coding on the lamp and it moved up out of the sand just a little. She started to rub her ear against the side of it, then used her head and neck and the entire side of her body. Long strokes of brushing against the side of the lamp, until—

The lamp began to glow and shake. A loud boom rang from the lamp as smoke began to come out of the spout. The little kitten jumped into the air and landed back down on all four legs, frozen in terror.

Out popped a genie!

"Master, what is your wish?" the genie said as it looked down at the kitten.

"Meow???"

THE MAGIC OF GRANDMA'S PANCAKES

McKel Jensen

"Girls! Come quick!" Grandma said.

When we ran to the kitchen, we saw her standing at the sliding glass window facing the backyard pointing.

"Look there," she said, stooping down to our level and directing our attention outside.

She knew exactly what would make her little granddaughters smile.

My parents would often drop my sister and me at my grandmother's house for the weekend. My grandmother was a master in the kitchen. She spent hours watching cooking shows on her television or cutting out recipes from cooking magazines. She would never try most of the recipes, but the simple act of clipping out something she could try showed that she was studying her craft.

Grandma lived in the foothills of Bountiful, Utah, beneath the big, white V on the mountain that represents Viewmont High School. Her house was built in the 1960's with white bricks and a light blue awning. My favorite part of the exterior of the house was a five-foot tall brick wall built outside the front bay window that was probably for privacy, but now seemed an arbitrary décor choice for the house. We used it as a playground, trying to climb onto the ledge and walk across the top like the balance beam in our gymnastics class.

Grandma's house had a huge carport where she would park her brown "tuna boat" car on one side. And since she didn't have a second car—as Grandpa passed away before I was born—she used the other side as a shady spot to put her white folding chair and watch over her quiet cul-de-sac. At the back of the carport, there was a small window that peered into the kitchen. Because the carport was higher than the house, a small girl like me could peek over the kitchen sink window and watch the activity inside.

When my mom's two sisters were in town, that kitchen was always busy. At sixteen, when the family was preparing to feed all who came to Grandma's funeral, I busied my helpless hands with making an apple pie that wasn't on the menu. "What is McKel doing?" My Aunt Karen asked. This act must have made an impression on her because she later bought me the book *How to Make a Pie* for my birthday.

That was the last time we used the kitchen and cooked together as a family.

Although Grandma was skilled in many things such as quilting and sewing, nothing could compete with her cooking. Of course, we all benefited from that skill. While a baby or newlywed might profit from a new quilt, everyone could benefit from her cooking. Grandma always made the most delicious meals. When my sister, Nicole, and I would visit, she would always make us pancakes for breakfast. Nicole and I may have been too young to appreciate her abilities beyond her pancake making skills—which, I'm quite positive were made from that yellow-boxed, premixed brand—but, we LOVED Grandma's pancakes. We definitely loved them more than we loved our dad's Saturday morning pancakes, which tradition ended abruptly that one time he added corn and we fired him.

Grandma's pancakes may not have been from scratch (and absolutely did not contain whole kernel corn), but we loved them and she always, always made more than our two little bellies could hold. At the end of our meal, she would open up the sliding glass door that faced her backyard and lead us onto the back porch. Because Nicole was older, she already knew what Grandma had intended, so Grandma took my hand and helped me tear up the leftover pancakes. I gave my sister a sideways glance as if to say, "This is crazy!"

With our little arms, we threw small chunks of our breakfast with all our might onto the grass and watched them land about a foot in front of us. *We never do this at home*, I thought. Mom would never allow it. This was why going to Grandma's was the best. We got to do things here that Mom wouldn't allow, even tearing up pancakes and throwing them on the lawn. Never questioning *why*, I knew that if my sister and Grandma were doing this, this must be a pretty cool thing to do.

After the crumbs from the plate were gone, we would go back into Grandma's maple-scented kitchen, close the glass door, and go about doing our own things—watching cartoons, play with the pedals on the organ, or investigating the contents of the record player that was both a music playing device and a gigantic piece of furniture. We could only assume that Grandma was just cleaning up breakfast, but a few minutes, or an hour, passed and Grandma called us to the kitchen.

"Girls! Come quick!" she hollered.

When we arrived, we saw her standing at the back door pointing at our torn-up pancakes.

"Look!" she said.

Half a dozen black birds were eating our pancakes! I gasped and giggled at seeing the magic that Grandma's pancakes made. "Birds eat pancakes, too!" I thought.

Years later I would try to create that same magic in my backyard, without Grandma. I learned to make pancakes by myself (because my dad was still fired), and after making a little extra, I went out to out on our suburbia Salt Lake City patio. The sky was blue, the grass was still dewy, and the air had only begun to warm. Having assured myself that I had followed the same steps as my grandma, I tore the pieces of pancake and threw them on our grass. Then I went back inside and waited. I kept myself busy with crayons, or some glittery craft project and would occasionally peek out to look for the birds. Maybe it's the city birds, my lack of patience, or that the egg/milk ratio in the batter was not right, but all I know is that I didn't have Grandma's magic and I would probably get in trouble for attracting ants and get fired. I wonder if this magic is hereditary, and perhaps skipped my generation.

MY LOVE

Steve Odenthal

I SIT ALONE,
Head in hand
A beaten hulk
Too weak to stand
The day had spent and laid me low
Its painful end, the final blow
Solitude is all I sought
To nurse these wounds of battles fought
And lost

But once again you bring the light
For your touch alone can make things right
Pulling me up and teaching anew
Kindling my spirit, with a new point of view
Tomorrow will be better, you promise me this
Then we smile together and life is bliss
We wish

But a promise does not always make it so
Pure love won't tame the winds, that much I know
Each day I battle and some days I win
For I have your love at each day's begin
And though it's thin armor, it gives me the might
To battle great dragons till with you tonight
My love

THE SHADOW TAKER

Valerie Odenthal

WHEN GRANDMOTHERS tell their grandchildren about the village of Chellidorie, it is often told as if it were a delicate blue robin's egg at the bottom if a woven nest. Others speak of it as if it were a gold coin pushed against the wrinkled furrows of an old man's hand. Yet many describe the laughter as a rainbow bubble floating toward the clouds. All of these would be true.

But, there was one in outside shadows of this joyous village that sought comfort amongst the walls of a dark and damp cave.

Laughter, giggles, and an occasional snort, echoed from the hills around the village. The children, all bare-footed and grass-stained, were rolling down the green hills that wrapped around their homes. Head over heels or cartwheeling down, maybe tummy up then belly down, one after the next. All found their way to the bottom of the sloping hill. They played in the meadow by their somersaulting playground. The hill was their magic slide. Joy. Bright and wonderful joy!

The day the butterfly flew through the village brought a great change into the lives of the children. This was a laughing, playing, and tumbling fun day. Then came a huge, brilliant, blue-winged wonder gliding over the heads of giggling children. The butterfly floated just beyond the reach of eager fingers, darting up and down as new colors attracted its attention, unaware of the gaggle of children in pursuit. Giggles and gasps confettied the air as the group ran after this beloved butterfly.

Racing up the pebble-lined paths into the hills, the group reached a stream weaving its way through the greenery. They had discovered a waterfall! The pond beneath cooled the bare feet of the children. Splashes and ripples of water took the focus of their adventure from the pursuit of the butterfly. As the tallest boy stepped back on shore, a mysterious hand reached from behind a large bush and *SNATCH!*

Minutes later, two smaller girls sat at the pond's edge resting and giggling when … *SNATCH!*

Again, the freckle-faced boy with a frog in hand crawled along the pond's edge chasing a second frog when … *SNATCH!*

Finally, the very tall girl noticed the brilliant blue butterfly as it landed on a yellow flower. Reaching for its azure wings when … *SNATCH!*

Unaware of what was taken, the tall girl scrambled after the brilliant butterfly and all the children joined back into the chase. Realizing that the sun was beginning to set, she knew it was time to head back to the village. A day of laughter and fun left the children hungry and ready to devour their dinners. Off they went skipping back along pebbled paths.

Upon realizing something was off, the tall girl stopped suddenly on the path. She shrieked! All of the children froze mid-step. Her shadow was gone! Other children looked to the path to see if they too were shadowless. Five children were missing shadows. As the sun was setting, others had shadows stretching out from their toes. For the victims of the *SNATCH* there were no such stretching images. What had happened?

Off the gaggle of children ran toward the village of Chellidorie with a mystery to solve. Shadows had been *SNATCHED!* Who would do such a thing? One voice over the next as the children told the story of the butterfly, waterfall, and a lovely day ending without shadows. Fear wrapped its web around the entire village and its families.

The twins, Aidan and Brooklyn, with all the energy of their six years of life, wanted to know what had happened to the shadows. They were so relieved they still had their own, but someone had to help their shadowless friends. Working together, discussing every evidence, the two concluded that the blue butterfly must have taken the shadows. So early the next morning, off they went to find the butterfly and the missing shadows.

Aidan carried a mesh net, and Brooklyn brought a clay jar to hold the blue-winged foe captive. Following the pebbled path past the tumbling hill, on they searched for the elusive, winged, would-be thief of shadows. There on the colorful flowers was a hint of blue. They ran toward the flutter of azure. *Yes!* It was the shadow-taking butterfly! In pursuit, the twins scurried after their target. It flew away through a maze of forest trees.

The twins ran off the path and through the forest. It wasn't until they found themselves in the shadows of large pines, that they realized they had never been there before. With fear of being lost, they looked for their villain.

Blue! Blue wings fluttered just a few feet away from them. Quietly they tip-toed closer, but off flew the butterfly. Running, they were in a chase with the shadow taker—up a steep hill then to more wildflowers with colors they had never even imagined, but the blue creature flew on. The twins scampered as quickly as their feet would go, tripping and scraping knees yet determined to make things right.

Then, just when they were worried that the butterfly might elude them, they saw its wings flutter into a dark cave. Aidan and Brooklyn looked at each other. They had never seen such a place before. What dangers could it hold?

Carefully they peeked in to see if the butterfly was near the entrance. Brooklyn readied her clay jar in case Aidan's net was successful. Quietly, they moved forward. Each step was slippery as the floors and walls of this place were damp and mossy.

Stop! There was the very butterfly they sought! But, it was not the butterfly that caused them to hault. It was not the blue wings that made their eyes wide with wonder. It was the shadows. Shadows in the shapes of their friends. The elongated or squatty shapes danced on the walls of this dark place, the fire burning in the center of the cave making the shadows look strange and eerie. But, stranger still was a large rounded being laughing and singing. This being had its back to the cave entrance and had not seen the twins as they entered. The shadows were playing with this creature.

Brooklyn gasped. The creature quickly turned to look at the startled pair whose faces grew pale at the sight of a real ogre standing in front of them.

"Get away from my shadow friends!" he bellowed.

The twins almost ran in fear, but Aidan bravely answered, "Those are the shadows of our friends. They do not belong to you. You are a … *SNATCHER!*"

"Give us back the shadows!" Brooklyn added.

To their surprise, the ogre began to cry. The twins' fear melted away.

"Why are you crying?" Aidan asked.

The ogre wiped his nose on his arm. Brooklyn moved closer. She patted the ogre on his other arm.

"Are you okay?" she asked.

"If you take the shadows back, I will be alone and have no friends," replied the distraught ogre.

Aidan began to smile.

The ogre looked at him strangely. "Do you think it is funny that I feel sad?"

"Oh no. No indeed," Aidan said. "You must come with us to the village of Chellidorie. Bring the shadows back to our friends. YOU need to come be OUR FRIEND!"

The three of them cheered and both children hugged their new friend as he agreed to this plan.

Aidan extended his mesh net as the ogre gathered the shadows. Once collected, Aidan let the ogre carry the cargo, as the shadows were much heavier than expected. Brooklyn skipped down the pebbled path toward the village. The blue-winged butterfly, who was the ogre's only friend before the shadow-taking, lead this unusual group back to the village.

At first, the villagers were alarmed to see the ogre with two children. They were ready to fight, but when the twins explained that the ogre had returned the shadows, there was a great celebration. Once the children had their shadows restored, the villagers began to dance around a bonfire. Food, laughter, and great joy again echoed from the hills around Chellidorie. The six-year-old twins, Aidan and Brooklyn, were heroes. The village gained a new friend and protector. And the blue butterfly showed the village children where to find the most beautiful flowers they had ever seen. No more *SNATCH!* And yes, they all lived Happily Ever After.

TEARS OF A CLOWN

Betti Avari

A TEAR SLIPS down my cheek, then another. Standing in Mom's bathroom—well, mine now—I study the lines at the corners of my eyes. They are the evidence of too many tears shed.

Probably permanent damage.

I reach for a tissue, then remember I'm out of tissues. And dangerously low on toilet paper—more evidence of my delicate emotional state. I haven't gone out in weeks, and until now I've managed to get by on freezer meals, ramen, powdered milk, and cereal. As a result of my "hermitude," a phrase I've coined for my sequestered existence, I look sallow, pale, and for nineteen, aged.

As my reflection brings a fresh wave of tears, I reach for Mom's chenille bathrobe, still hanging on the bathroom door, and press it to my face. Then I curl into a ball at the foot of Mom's robe, wrapping it around me like a tent.

Cocooned in the robe's embrace, I feel truly safe. Through the haze of my perpetual grief, one of last week's podcasts comes to mind. It said that nobody understands loss until they've lived it. Or was that podcast from *two* weeks ago? Either way, I've started rationalizing that somebody understands. "I'm not alone," I moan. "I'm not alone!"

Even as I say it, I know it's foolish. The truth is, at this point, I don't just live loss, I AM loss. I could live another lifetime without any more loss and still feel gypped.

First, my sister Maren, killed in a freak highway accident when her elbow hit the driver's side window button and the resulting wind caused my twelfth-birthday-party balloons to fly into her face.

Then Dad and Mom split. He just couldn't forgive my mom for asking Maren to pick the balloons up in the first place. Mom begged Dad to attend even one counseling session, but he refused. He died that Christmas, of intentional causes.

I press my cheek to the cold tile floor.

The tears are streaming now, and my face is hot.

It must suck to die, but it may suck a little more to be left behind.

Mom tried so hard to stick around for me. She found a temp job after Dad left, cooked homemade meals still, and took me to the library, like, all the time. "Cheap fun," she'd call it. Even after dad died, she kept her chin up. But I knew that deep inside she was slowly crumbling, and not just from the cancer that took her life the week before my high school graduation.

Now, I'm the one that's crumbling. I only bother blotting my eyes dry today because I'm going out. Contact with the human race!

Well, almost human.

I stand and face my reflection once more. With Mom's bronzer brush in hand, I try to compensate for a summer sequestered indoors. Stroke after stroke, I paint myself happy. I have to, or Cassie will have me institutionalized.

An hour later, I'm in Cassie's black Honda, sunroof open and radio up. The sun's too bright, the noise too jarring. I want to go home.

I adjust my sunglasses, and Cassie shoots me a look. "You look like a vampire. Like Death without the sharp hook-thing."

"Scythe." I sigh. "Where are you taking me?"

"It's a surprise. It's on my bucket list, so you might be able to guess—I don't know. I just know that animal rights activists are screwing with the possibility of...gah! I almost told you!"

"You told me enough." I dig my nails into my palms. I want to jump from the moving car and crawl on hands and knees the whole way home—to safety and peace and quiet. Even institutionalization sounds great at this point. The alternative is much more painful. "C'mon, Cassie! The circus?" I groan.

"Not just any circus, The Shadow Circus!" she squeals. "The tent has blacklights and stuff."

"Ooh!"

I feign excitement while we walk through the steamy, sun-baked fairgrounds, but when we reach the small ticket booth I balk at the cost of admission. "Twenty dollars? Remind me why I'm subjecting myself to this torture!"

Cassie's expression remains cool. "Because you're a dork in need of a social life. Don't you have your mom's life insurance yet?"

I shield my face with my wallet and swat at a fly with my free hand.

I haven't followed up on Mom's life insurance yet. Haven't gone to the mailbox once. I'm surprised that I have running water and electricity at this point. I know that it's depression. I know that I should reach out to a doctor, a social worker—anyone!—but I just can't bring myself to search for a phone number and dial. I sniff. "Do you actually think my cure for depression is getting close and personal with people who have to paint their smiles on?"

Cassie shrugs. "I don't know why people are scared of them. Clowns are hot. Pennywise is kinda cute, don't you think?"

I shake my head. "I give up. You're hopeless."

"Speaking of hopeless," Cassie pokes me as we walk past an overweight clown who's scratching his butt as he walks. She leans in and whispers, "See? Hot. You could have missed out on the sights."

Sarcasm is always a precursor to a major Cassie outburst.

"Uh-huh." I swallow a mouthful of stale-popcorn air. But Cassie's in a mood already, and holding my breath won't help.

Not one bit.

"Come one, come all!" she exclaims, "To the hottest striptease this side of Vegas! Carnal Carnies! See it to believe it, folks! No safety net."

"Stop it," I growl. "You're being obnoxious."

"Hey, YOLO! It's no biggie."

"No. I don't think 'you only live once,' Cassie. In fact, I think reincarnation is a very real thing for people that act like dung beetles in this life."

I squirm as we hand our money to the shadiest ticket vendor in existence.

Cassie's too busy smiling at the ticket man to pay attention to me. It's almost a hundred degrees in the sun, but the way he looks us up and down? It makes me wish I'd worn something less revealing. A shiver runs down my spine as he grips my hand to press a red stamp to my wrist.

I catch up to Cassie. "Man, he's creepy!"

Cassie shoots him a wink as we hurry through the turnstile.

"You know, someday you just might regret your actions," I hiss. "You think life's a game? It's not. It's serious! Karma catches up to people."

She grabs my arm. "I know! The trick is to outrun it!"

She starts running, dragging me along till I forget my fear and the way my atrophied muscles refuse to work properly. Giggling, we race to the tent door. As my eyes adjust to the darkness and I catch my breath, I see that there are less than thirty people in the stands. Cassie races to the front row and throws herself onto the bench.

"Front and center? Seriously, Cass?"

She shrugs and pats the bench beside her. "Go big or go home!"

I slide in beside her. "And how is this place going to help my depression?"

"You get to hang with your bestie." Cassie shrugs. "That's good enough, isn't it? It's been two months since our last get together."

"Two?" I sigh for more than one reason. One, I don't know what month it is. Two, "get together" is Cassie speak for my mom's funeral. I stare at the elephant swaying in a narrow pen just outside the arena. It probably doesn't know what day it is, either.

"You know?" Cassie wraps her arm around my shoulders. "I forgive you for not calling. You probably needed to go through her stuff and sort it all out. I hear those things take time."

I haven't sorted anything. I've left it all the same, from the medicines on Mom's bedside table to the drug schedule on the fridge. I only consumed her pudding cups and protein drinks out of sheer necessity. I really don't want to discuss this at all, especially not at some stupid circus, so I change the subject.

"How are your parents?" It's a low blow, even if I *am* deflecting.

A mixture of affairs and prescription drug abuse elevated Cassie's family closer to a three-ring circus than this sad little outfit.

"Still divorced, thank you very much."

"How long has it been now? Two years? And I thought they were getting back together." I roll my eyes in mock-sarcasm.

She sticks out her tongue. "Blah, blah, blah." Then her eyes light up. "Hey, you think my life's a nightmare? I think it's time you start a horror show of your very own. Get a boyfriend, pop out a few kids?"

"Families aren't horror shows."

"Mine is." She points toward the arena. "See that little clown in the purple getup? He has 'Baby Daddy' written all over him!"

I turn. In the arena just a few yards away from us is a man with dwarfism, dressed in a purple clown suit and colorful wig. He's pulling a wooden platform into position.

Cassie whoops, "Oh, yeah! It's on! I'm getting his number after the show. You can have lots of little midget babies! Start a circus of your own!" She's laughing hysterically.

But I feel guilty for setting her off. "Seriously, Cassie! Knock it off. That word's offensive. What if he heard you?" As I try to shush her, I can see that the damage is already done.

The clown turns, and his chin juts in the air as he glares at us. His thick, painted smile can't cover his anger.

"Cassie!" I beg. "Stop."

"Who cares?" Cassie laughs.

"People, Cass. Just … people." To the left, a young mother shakes her head and tries to distract her children from the scene. To the right, some young boys with licorice ropes around their necks stare at us, jaws agape. But Cassie's laughing so hard that she can't see through her tears.

She's spiraling out of control, and I can't stop it.

Gratefully, the clown's a pro. His scowl turns to a smile to match his makeup as he steps onto the platform and pulls at his wig. When it doesn't budge, he shrugs comically. The kids in the audience laugh.

"See?" Cassie hisses. "He's just a clown! He's here for a laugh."

"What's he going to say, Cass?"

"I know, I know!" Cassie bellows. "He's gonna tell me that the show's got enough clowns for this act? Maybe he'll tell me to—wait for it—stop clowning around!" She slaps her thigh.

The clown tugs harder on his rainbow wig. Still, no result.

The licorice rope gang starts laughing as the clown's expression takes on a frustrated quality. It really looks like he's trying to pull his wig off in earnest. His fists are clenched, and he's banging his head to and fro. It's a pathetic, defeated gesture. The audience isn't close enough to see his pained expression, his muscles straining in earnest, the sudden tear that slides down his cheek as he stops trying.

That's when it hits me. He's stuck in a show just like I am.

I feel a bond with this man. Cassie has to stop. I'm about to warn her about karma and dung beetles again, but the clown is staring at us, and he's rolling his sleeves up his tan arms.

I wave apologetically at the clown, but he keeps staring at Cassie.

I feel my smile fade as his expression hardens.

The clown points two fingers at Cassie, then grabs a fistful of the wig. The wig falls effortlessly from his bare scalp, and the clown's eyes widen. He puts both hands to his head in surprise as the wig falls to the dust. Suddenly, a loud laugh escapes from his painted mouth, maniacal and high-pitched, and his oversized shoes pound the platform as he jumps up and down excitedly.

Jumps and gasps erupt from the surprised audience.

Then Cassie busts out laughing, too. Her pitch almost matches his. In all our years as friends, she's never laughed like that before. It's so loud that the audience doesn't know where to look, shuffling glances between the clown and Cassie.

The clown's laughter dies down, but not Cassie's, so he just looks at me and shrugs sadly as he bends to retrieve the wig. Then he bows, his butt to the audience in true clown fashion. He doesn't look back as he walks away on his stocky legs. His head is hung low, and he's wringing the wig in his hands.

"What a show!" someone gasps. The audience cheers and begins to clap, but my hands are at my throat.

This didn't feel like an act. Not entirely, anyway. I'm sure clowns must use good glue to keep their wigs in place, but his effort looked genuine.

"What just happened? Cassie?"

She looks at me in surprise, like she's forgotten I'm there.

I know Cassie. She's all fun and games, even if she goes too far. My mom knew it, too, but the clown didn't. Cassie's fun usually lightens the dark times. She even called my mom "Uni-boober" after her mastectomy—

straight to her face—till the end. And Mom loved it because she understood that Cassie coped with laughter. That's always been her way. Even if the humor comes at another's expense.

Cassie's crazy laughing finally dies down to a long sigh, and she wipes the tears from her eyes.

"Are you crying?" I ask in disbelief. "What's gotten into you? Let's go get some popcorn. Maybe a clown nose for you?"

She shrugs and follows.

I fork over eight dollars for a bag of popcorn at the concession stand. By then, Cassie's deflated like a helium balloon, all used up to make someone's voice higher for a moment. Her little act was an attempt at an equally temporary happiness.

I pass the popcorn to her. "They don't have any clown noses, weirdo."

We sit on a concrete curb beside a canal and pinch pieces of popcorn out of the bag in silence. Mom used to call us "little squirrels" when we ate popcorn like this.

"Cassie, I'm sorry I've been so withdrawn."

Cassie nods. "Me, too. Pulling away wasn't fair to you. I've been dealing with depression again, and other stuff, but that doesn't mean I don't love you."

"I know. You're my best friend. And, I hate to admit it, but I've felt more alive in the last hour than I have in the past month." Or two. I pause and take a deep breath. "Cassie?"

"Hmm?"

"I think you should move in with me."

Her eyes light up. "Really?" she squeals. She throws her arms around me, and the popcorn spills as she starts laughing. It's that crazy clown laugh again. "Leave my ghetto apartment for the burbs? Roomies?"

I shrug. "I've got the whole house to myself now. All I ask is that you help me keep the bills paid. And, most of all, you have to promise to be nice to the little people."

"But—"

I level a serious glare at her. "Take it or leave it."

Circus introduction music blares from the speakers behind us, and Cassie pouts for a second in mock-frustration. Then a genuine smile lights her face. "Deal!"

"Do you want to watch the show?"

"Nah." She stands up and offers me her hand. "Circuses are overrated. I just brought you here so you'd ask me to move in with you. That's on my bucket list, too."

I giggle. "Weirdo. Just ask next time."

As we trudge back to the dusty parking lot, we make plans to move her in next week.

I've got a lot of housework to do.

We reach her car and do a double take. Her black car is covered in dust, but the other cars are clean. The words, "Let's laugh!" are drawn in the dust in neat lowercase letters on the driver's side door. A rainbow-colored clown wig rests on the hood.

"This is great," Cassie grins. She grabs the wig and pulls it over her head. "How do I look?" She laughs.

"Like a real clown." I can't help my skeptical expression. "Who did this?"

She giggles. "Who cares!"

"Time for a carwash?" I ask.

"Sure, but I'm keeping the wig." She wears it as she drives me back to my house. I don't mind the sun or the noise anymore.

Three days later, I knock on her door, pizza in hand. "It's Friday night, weirdo. Let's get you packed!" There isn't an answer. "Cassie! Don't tell me you've changed your mind."

I hear shuffling feet, the turn of the knob. Then the door opens, just a crack, and the footsteps shuffle away again.

"Cassie?"

Her apartment is pitch black. I don't remember where the light switch is in the large loft space, so I feel along the exposed brick as I step inside. "Cassie," I growl. "This isn't funny."

I hear a giggle to the left of the door. "But I'm so good at laughs."

It's Cassie's voice, for sure, but it sounds—different.

"What's going on?" I try to not sound nervous, because that's what Cassie wants.

As my eyes adjust to the orange glow of the streetlight streaming in from the window, I set the pizza on the couch and reach into my pocket for my phone. My flashlight cuts through the dark as I pan the room.

I catch sight of the wig Cassie wore home from the circus. It hangs in the corner of the room.

"Where are you?"

Her voice echoes off the brick wall. "I don't know."

"Where's the light switch? I can't remember where it's at in this place."

"Beside the sink." Giggle.

I march to the kitchen and flip the switch. Blinking in the light, I look around and come up empty. There's no sign of her.

In the back of the loft, I catch a movement out of the corner of my eye. The clown wig is moving toward me slowly, suspended in the air.

"I'm not in the mood for pranks, Cassie," I warn. I run at the wig, intent on ripping it from the fishing line or whatever is holding it up. Instead, I find myself on the ground in a tangle, having collided with something … "Cassie?"

The wig nods. "Oh, my gosh! Can you still feel me?" She laughs in surprise. The same crazy, high-pitched laugh she and the circus clown shared.

I feel her arms wrap around me in a tight hug, but all I can see is that wig. This close to it, I can see that it's been mangled, cut and shaved in places. "Uh, what's going on?"

Dread fills the pit of my stomach. She's actually invisible.

"I don't know!" Again, she giggles. "I tried to take the wig off after I got home from the circus, but I couldn't. It was stuck to my head. Like the wig grew into my brain. I tried cutting it off, tried plucking it out … tried everything!" She laughs. "Don't think I haven't tried everything."

"A blowtorch?"

There's a pause. Then another giggle. "I'm afraid it might come to that."

"You're kidding. . ." This whole situation is unreal.

"I think the wig is cursed." She chuckles. "I can only see myself in the dark, and what I see isn't good. I'm changing. I can't even talk without laughing!" She guffaws.

Her laughter is out of place with the situation, and a sudden flashback fills my mind, a vision of that clown bursting into laughter and looking surprised by it.

Cassie is really in trouble.

She keeps giggling. Then, mind reading again, she says, "I think I royally pissed that clown off. They always have those smiles painted on. . .maybe not so trustworthy after all." I feel her release me. The wig floats up and across the room to the kitchen.

"Cassie." I choke back my tears. "We've got to take it off!"

"I think it's too late." She laughs as the lights go out.

"What are you doing?" I cry.

"Calm down, silly." She giggles. "I just want you to see what's happening to me. So you understand how serious this is. Come to the window."

My eyes adjust, and when I can see the window again, I stand and follow the sound of her voice.

Her laughter is higher pitched than before. "Maybe people like me aren't reincarnated into dung beetles . . ."

I see the wig floating in the orange streetlight and reach for it.

She catches my hand midair and rests my palm below the wig, against her cheek. "Do you see?" Her voice echoes off the window pane. "Do you see what I mean?"

She turns her face toward me, nods up and down, and I catch sight of an iridescent shimmer. I will my eyes to see, and eventually, a shape comes forth from the darkness.

"Cassie?" I wail.

Her face is gaunt, her eyes have sunken into hollow sockets. A large, toothy grin is etched in vibrant colors across her skin. There's a sheen to it, like oil, but I can't rub it off her face. I try a little harder.

"Believe me," she sighs with a giggle. "I've tried all of that. The face paint gets brighter and brighter every day, as I disappear into the shadows more and more. I can't escape it."

"What, like, the Shadow Circus cursed you? Is that what I'm supposed to believe?" A tear slips down my cheek, then another. I stop rubbing her face and start caressing it instead. "You were going to move in with me! We were going to be there for each other …"

"I know." She laughs. "I'm so, so sorry!"

I find myself reaching upward. I grab a fistful of those rainbow-colored curls and tug.

"Geez!" she exclaims. "Like I said—he-he!—I think it's my hair now. Remember the words on my dusty car?"

"Um, something about laughter."

"'Let's laugh!' That's what it said. That clown is getting his revenge."

"No," I gasp. "It can't be! This isn't you!" I picture her blonde hair swaying like fields of golden wheat as we ran through the circus in the sunlight. "You were just messing around! I'm taking you to the emergency room."

"It's permanent."

"Cassie, no!" I cry.

A tear slides down Cassie's cheek. "It's getting worse," she moans. "There's nothing I can do. I'm sorry!"

A cold chill spreads through me.

"You warned me, but I didn't listen!" She giggles. "Apparently, the show had enough room for one more clown after all. I guess it's better than a dung beetle, but karma still sucks. You don't deserve to be alone!"

"Cassie," I sob.

"I'm so …" Her painted smile grimaces as she says the last words I ever hear her speak.

The wig drops to the floor, and she vanishes for good.

"… sorry?"

I finish the phrase for her, then slowly back away. I catch sight of my movement in the reflection of the window and turn to face it. Once again, my tears are my only company. They're the tears of a clown stuck in a circus I don't want any part of, because I'm alone again.

I glance down at the wig. It lies at my feet, in the shadows. I stare incredulously at it. Then I bend over to retrieve it, gently, to preserve the magic.

And I put it on.

THE LURE OF PUMPKIN PIE

Valerie Odenthal

PERCHED ON THE edge of a cedar chest, now used as a dining bench in my Grandma and Grandpa Mangum's kitchen, my feet dangled above the floor. Squirming side to side to find a spot to survey the feast before me, I wiggled closer to the edge. My cousins squished together on this family heirloom. With giggles, pokes, and laughter, we all found a suitable seat. Only a short distance away was a warm home baked pumpkin pie! The reminder that "real" food must be eaten before dessert was even considered, redirected my young gaze. So the feasting began. Homemade rolls with Grandma's best jams were within reach. There was a savory ham topped in pineapple rings and brown sugar. In the middle of the feast was a golden turkey with its steam curling up past the creamy mashed potatoes in thick turkey gravy, wiggly gelatin salads, and all manner of garden-grown vegetables all sharing a kaleidoscope of colors. My favorite "real food" was the sticky toasted marshmallow-topped candied yams. A harvest setting of a summer of farming in the mountains of Southern Utah for Thanksgiving were displayed beautifully at our fingertips. The pumpkin pie was the end goal.

Bits and pieces of turkey, salads, mashed potatoes, and other traditional foods were eaten between stories, laughter, and the sway of a family moving together in a dance without music. The siren call of the warm pie begged me to power through the plate of food before I could answer.

Suddenly, spirals of terra cotta colored goo flew through the air. Faces, clothing, and dinnerware dripped with the warm pumpkin filling. Gasp! There in the pumpkin pie, bull's eye center, was "Rudolph" the trophy mount mule deer head. This prize relic from a hunt taken by my Grandpa, a decor piece that while large, was so familiar in his presence, that it had been completely ignored. His red Christmas wrap foil nose was buried in the center of the now splattered pumpkin pie. Fortunately, nothing more than a few tipped water glasses resulted from the flying antlered taxidermy-ed buck head, but the pie was gone.

Lacking the proper Olympic score cards for this amazing spiral dive, we resorted to vocal score keeping. Definitely damage worthy of a score of a perfect 10!

The lure of the pumpkin pie was too great for Rudolph. He beat me to my pie! The wink of his glass eye, with its mischievous twinkle, let me know he won this round.

RECEIVING AUTUMN

Alice M. Batzel

AUTUMN CAME and quietly sat beside me.
I spent a bit of time with her,
and so enjoyed her company.
We never spoke a word,
but what a rich connection we had,
just she and I.

She shared with me a panorama of colors
beyond any artist's palette, hues light and dark,
vibrant and soft: burgundy, burnt sienna,
saffron yellow, and rusted orange,
a feast of nature's paintbrush before my eyes.

I inhaled the cold evening and watched leaves
of crimson and gold gently fall from branches.
The breeze enticed them to dance.
We sat in silence, Autumn and I.
She gifted me a meditative communion.

The scent of nearby harvest apples tickled my nose.
A chilly wind kicked the leaves about my feet
and whistled in my ears.
The sun slowly dropped below the horizon
withdrawing its warmth, and I shivered.

Somewhere in the evening air, I thought I heard a whisper,
"Remember me, dear friend, I'll soon be gone."
I silently promised, "I'll watch for you again next year.
Your memory blazes within me, a grand gift like no
other."

WE DON'T DARN SOCKS!

Steve Odenthal

IN MY HOME, there is one ironclad rule. It is a simple one. We Don't Darn Socks! I mean, ever! Such practices will forever be forbidden in any domicile I inhabit.

I realize that to others this does not seem like a bolt of lightning out of the blue. No, indeed, very few husbands, wives, or significant others do such handmaiden-like repairs in this disposable day and age. I am positive that it is a rare fellow (or woman for that matter) who has ever been so bothered by a hole to have even considered taking up needle and thread. Today, it is simpler to go out and buy a new pair of socks when a heel or toe makes an unplanned appearance.

Don't mistake my meaning; I am not complaining here. In fact, the No Darning rule came into being at *my* request. This rule was made as a matter of self-preservation and should not be looked at as a reflection upon anyone's homemaking skills. My wife is quite capable of this type of repair. I just simply will not let her do it—no way, no how, not hardly.

My attitude is: "Socks worn down and threadbare? Not standing as tall as you did yesterday? No problem. Toss those nasty things away and break out a new pair. For that matter, if it is warm enough to get by without socks—hey! Wear sandals. Loosen up!"

That's how I feel today, but I did not always have this attitude. When my wife and I were first married, oh so many years ago, we lived a very frugal existence as starving college students. We were very good at it...*starving* that is. To prevent extreme weight loss, every nickel, every dime was thoroughly and lovingly caressed before leaving our hand. Believe me, between counting out our coins and giving them a farewell kiss, we were never crowd favorites in express checkout lines. Sadly, we always wound up there, as we seldom could afford more than ten items at any one time.

Back in those days, a new pair of socks would have been carefully contemplated, budgeted, and then, most likely, placed on layaway. It became a race to see which came first, the last payment to the store or my big toe fully exposing itself through the cotton. Normally, the toe won. Oh, we tried to negotiate. (With the store, not the toe.) I was usually stuck wearing a sock with a hole for a while.

The very thought of this was more than my loving bride could bear. She set about to provide a fix for the sad situation, meeting the challenge of domesticity with great enthusiasm. She grabbed a needle and thread, and then started sewing on everything in sight. In addition to socks, she tried her hand at sheets, shirts, shorts, sweaters, and other things—even items whose names did not begin with the letter *S*—like curtains and cupboards. Oh yes, this Domestic Goddess stuff went to her head and she actually embroidered our initials on the kitchen cabinets. I kind of liked it, however, the landlady was less than pleased.

As you can well imagine, I was happy. Not only did her efforts save us money, but my big toe once again enjoyed the warmth and comfort that its brothers felt, sitting snugly, submerged beneath an unblemished cotton cover. This was bliss. "Big toe bliss." This skill was the proverbial two birds with one stone. Not only were my feet warm, but we could now kiss off any remaining sock at the layaway department. This, my friends, was way cool. At least this was what passed for cool in the life of a couple of married and starving college kids.

Things went zipping by for the next few months. We were positively giddy with all the money we were saving on socks alone. (Hey, I have a hyperactive big toe, okay?) This new economy we were enjoying could not have come at a better time for us.

Our college traditionally held a special year-end concert. After our many hours of sacrifice and study, it was our shared dream to be able to attend this "happening" event. This particular year the college had been promoting the concert at every opportunity, but always with the promise that the main act would be a HUGE surprise. Before the money acquired through the Great Sock Savings Plan, we hadn't a prayer of being able to swing the tickets. Now it was a doable thing.

We purchased our tickets and got together with the other *way cool* people that frequented our little college campus. On the appointed night we made our way to the concert venue in the Center for the Performing Arts. I had spent a great many hours in this building—some of them actually in class—and I knew the back hallways like the back of my hand. We would use that advantage and arrive before the crowd.

This building was essentially a huge auditorium surrounded by great echoing halls with lots of empty classrooms. Each deserted room off the highly polished hallway beckoned to wandering students, promising an advanced course in mischief. To some meandering couples in this building, the course of study might change to an upper division Human Relations offering. Both the college and the custodial staff discouraged such matriculation. To that end, each night the staff diligently added layer upon layer of wax and shine to the floor in a job that never seemed to cease.

But on this night, we were there for fun, music, and laughter—not mischief. We were also there to find out the identity of the mysterious headlining act. Rumors were rampant across campus, but the secret was still safe, at least from our little group of party animals. Using my mental map of the venue, we beat the rest of the crowd and found a back corridor in the building. We made our way up the deserted hallway, echoing loudly, proudly turned out in our very best concert attire.

We were indeed a sight. *Stylin'* would be too moderate a description. We popped and jived up the polished corridor, reminiscent of jovial extras fresh from the *Starsky and Hutch* TV show. While we all wore platform shoes—because, you know, *Stylin'*—in this episode I had Huggy Bear's extra altitude shoes on. And I was loving it.

My wife and I were resplendent in matching metallic-sheen shirts and yes, she had sewn them herself. I was wearing tight, bright bell-bottom slacks that were also a recent creation of my lovely bride. To put it bluntly, we were not only *making the scene*, we *were* the scene … and it was HAPPENING!

As we styled up the hallway, a custodian was just finishing one last layer of shellac on the floor. He looked up as we approached him.

"Oh, great. It's gonna be Disco. I bet on the Doobies!" he grunted as he slopped the mop back into its bucket.

It was obvious the man was disappointed. Maybe not as disappointed as we were to hear him associate our group with Disco, but you could tell he wasn't pleased at the prospect of a night with the Village People.

He yelled to us as we passed, "Careful … it's slick!"

With that warning, he yanked on the cord of his floor buffer, hoping to remove it from our paths. Unfortunately, I took this to be a signal to leap over the top of the moving cord. In Huggy's shoes, my leaping was subpar and I landed not over, but exactly on top of the cord mid-flight. Not a good place to be, I thought to myself.

I'm sure that I would have moved to safety in that half-second had I not been distracted by the sudden emergence of at least one thousand other students, all ticket-holders, who spilled towards us from the far end of the hall. Obviously, someone had opened the gates and our group was no longer alone in the great hallway.

Huggy's shoes then began to dance. Okay, maybe *dance* is the wrong word. With me as their occupants, about the best these magic shoes could do was to run in place atop the cord, like a lumberjack in some northwest logrolling competition. It did not take long for me to topple off the cord. Instinctively I stretched out my right leg in a long stride to keep from falling all the way to the floor.

As I approximated the splits, a great pain came upon me. It was localized in the nether regions of my new slacks. I knew at once that the money saved on socks was not worth it. A wayward needle, left unintentionally in a threadbare sock had apparently endured both the wash and rinse cycle then navigated to the pants. Lying dormant up to this point, the sharp metallic object had been jostled to a new position by my sudden lumberjack-like movements and now had deflated my ego so to speak.

I gave a loud, gravelly voice to my pain without thought or care. "HHHHeeeeeyyyyaaaa! Help Me!" I yelled as my eyes rolled back in my head and I headed to the floor.

The situation was obvious to me. In my weakened condition, my right leg kept sliding forward. There was absolutely nothing that I could do about it. My descent continued and my eyes rolled back into place in my head but widened with uncontrolled fear as my brain realized what would come next—the splits. In my best day, I could not approach the splits. I also knew that a painful puncture would soon become a complete harpooning. For a split second, I mentally commiserated with Melville's great whale. I had felt his pain. Oh, how I hated Ahab!

I hit the floor and the worst indeed came, for I was reduced to a small, sweating, grunting little man in a shiny suit at the concert venue. All that I could muster in the way of understandable communication was the repeated loud and guttural plea, "Somebody Help Meee! Owww!"

My wife sized up the situation quickly. "I think he's torn his new pants! Let's get him up! But cover him first!" One of the members of my group instantly sacrificed style and pulled off his coat, which rivaled the one made famous by *Joseph* conspiring with Andrew Lloyd Webber. The blur of motion and light reflected from that cloak was stunning. However, my pain-induced reverie was cut short by the collective groans of the masses moving down the hall as they caught sight of our little entourage. The approaching herd had obviously noted my wife's flamboyant be-dazzling of our hipster attire. I heard them cry out as one, "Oh Man! I knew it! It *is* going to be Disco! No wonder they wouldn't tell us who the headliner was." The mob was obviously disgusted and had turned ugly. I knew I had to get to a safe place.

My friends, Starsky and Hutch, each took one arm, after throwing the coat over my shoulders to free their hands, and attempted to lift me to my feet. Their intention was good. To this day, I know that it was. But, in fairness, none of them had ever been on a whaling vessel, so they couldn't have known that moving a harpooned body is no fun for anyone involved.

My knees buckled. I was heading down again, sinking slowly. Through tear-glazed eyes, I helplessly surveyed the scene. I had not realized that the crowd at the end of the hallway were suddenly and quietly surrounding us. The pure number of spectators astounded me causing me to utter in my surprise and pain, "Good gaud, y'all!" This exclamation, like all my pained verbalizations thus far had, echoed deeply in those cavernous halls.

I tried to get myself to my feet and stand tall, throwing the coat from my shoulders—straining for the dignity of escaping under my own power. But, alas, the pain was too great and I slumped towards the floor again. Starsky caught me midway down and Hutch again covered me with the coat as we walked and buckled our way toward an empty classroom.

"Somebody Help Me! Owww!" I repeatedly cried out as we shambled to that safe haven.

The crowd seemed to mingle outside the closed classroom for a while as I extracted the offending needle, which proved to be a chore of unbelievable difficulty. I whimpered in a corner, trying my best to recover a normal vocal range. We could hear the hallway speculation through the door.

"I'm telling you it *is* James Brown, man!"

"No it's not, man. That wasn't him!"

"Man, I'd know his voice anywhere. It's James Brown, the Godfather of Soul!"

"Man! That guy was white! James Brown is black!"

"Oh, great! This school is so cheap they brought in an impersonator! What a rip!"

"What?" A new voice chimed in. "An Elvis Impersonator? Jeeze! What'd these tickets cost, again?"

"What a rip-off, Man! That guy didn't sound anything like Elvis!"

"I'm telling ya … it was James Brown! I've seen him do that cape thing at the end of his show before!"

The argument raged outside the door for a half-hour. Inside the classroom, all was quiet except for the occasional involuntary sob as I recovered. I learned that day who had my back. They still do. I couldn't let my lady and undercover cop-like friends down—we had to make the scene.

It was halfway through the Doobie Brothers' set by the time we sauntered in, shaken but still ready to rock. We made it through the night and the rest of the concert with no further costume malfunctions. It was truly a night to remember. But from that day forward a decree went out upon the land, and mark my words well, that in our home we will never, EVER darn socks again!

PUBLISHER'S ACKNOWLEDGEMENTS

MY SINCERE THANKS to the many people who helped make this anthology a reality. It started as a simple idea to share work from some of the talented writers involved in the Brigham City Writers chapter of the League of Utah Writers, but it quickly grew into a showcase of the wide variety of storytelling that comes from Northern Utah authors (and one from Idaho). Thank you to all our BCW members for supporting our chapter, and to the honorary members we've adopted from other chapters (you know who you are). Thank you McKel Jensen and David Cowsert for editing the prose alongside me, and to Felicia Rose for editing the poetry. A humble and forever-in-your-debt thank you to E.B. Wheeler for assisting in several aspects of this project and cover design.

A personal thank you to my partners in writerhood crime—the CWGuild. And of course, to my family who listened to me ramble about the odds and ends of this project for months. A writer may create in isolation, but there's always a loved one who reminds us when it's time to stop working and get some sleep. And that maybe we should eat something.

Keri Montgomery
Brigham City Writers Chapter President
Willow Park Press

ABOUT THE AUTHORS

Nestled within the peaks of Northern Utah, **BETTI AVARI** spends her sleepless nights tucked under a fuzzy blanket, typing out her latest nightmare. Writing is her coping mechanism. She admits, "I don't seek to add nightmares to this life—only a way through those that already exist. Believe in the beauty of your dreams . . . and nightmares!" She would be nowhere without Stephanie Gittins, The Clandestine Writerhood Guild, the Brigham City Writers, and her family's tireless support of her passion. Previous works are available in the Utah Horror Writers Anthologies: *The Hunger* and *Peak of Madness*.

ALICE M. BATZEL is a displaced beach writer from the Northwest Florida Gulf Coast living in the Rocky Mountains of Utah. She is a published author, playwright, journalist, poet, and freelance writer. Alice has published with Pioneer Drama Service, Inc., the JAHIMA of Chicago, Box Elder Magazine, the Utah Humor Anthology, and has been a guest writer with various newspapers. She studied at Utah State University, Northwest Florida State College, and the AHIMA of Chicago. Her western comedy/mystery stage script, *WHO SHOT THE SHERIFF?,* has been performed across the United States and Canada entertaining audiences, serving charity fundraising for pediatric trauma care, and providing financial support for high school drama programs and community theater organizations. Alice is a retired credentialed Health Information Management Specialist with a 32-year career in the acute care hospital setting, also serving as a patient rights advocate regarding end-of-life decision making, quality of care, and medical ethics. She is currently writing magazine articles, poetry, novels, stage scripts, and book reviews. Alice is married, the mother of two adult sons, and grandmother of five. She and her husband enjoy living in a peaceful rural community at the foot of a majestic mountain range in northern Utah.

KATHY DAVIDSON lives in a small town on the borders of Bear Lake with her husband and their large hound dog. She has novels on the brain so when her three kids were raised, she went back to school and earned a bachelor's degree in English so she could write. She took time out from working on her first novel to write short stories. Kathy belongs to the Brigham City Chapter and the Just Write Chapter.

MCKEL JENSEN holds a Master of Arts in English from Weber State University where she was selected to be the commencement speaker for her graduating class. She has won awards for her short story "Goblin Creek" and is proud to have her essay "Finding Muchness" published alongside nationally recognized essayists through Full Grown People. Her essay was selected to be part of a larger print anthology called *Soul Mates 101* under the same publisher. She has worked as a technical writer for manufacturing, pharmaceutical and government contracting companies. McKel lives in Brigham City with her husband and three adorable, attention-seeking young children.

RACHAEL JESSOP loves to write stories, to help her boys with their homework, and to teach her preschool children about the wonders in life. There's never a dull moment for her, with a home full of teaching, parenting, writing, art, children, animals, reading, EMS and fire responding, and love. Rachael took Second Honorable Mention at the 2018 League of Utah Writers Creative Writing Contest in the Children's Story Category. Busy writing and illustrating more stories, she is excited for her journey to progress.

Although she wrote her first 4-line poem before entering kindergarten, **DEDE MATTIX** never succumbed to the title of "poet" until taking a writing class taught by Professor Darrell Spencer at BYU in 1984. Since then, despite being sidetracked by the publication of a novel and several short stories, she continues to write and win awards for her poems and is currently at work on a chapbook.

KERI MONTGOMERY writes mainly middle grade and adult speculative fiction. She's a contributing author to *Rise Above Depression*, the former #1 Amazon bestseller in self-help by main author and inspirational speaker Jodi Orgill Brown. Keri's short fiction can be found in the 2019 Utah Horror Writers Association Anthology *Peaks of Madness*, in the 2018 LUW Press anthology *At First Glance*, and also in the 2019 LUW Press anthology *Metamorphosis*.

She's a board member for the League of Utah Writers and founder of the Brigham City Writers chapter. When not writing, she enjoys firefighting with her department, convincing her kids that museums are cool, and wishing for superhuman skills.

MIKE NELSON grew up on a small farm in northern Utah where he entertained himself with daydreams. A corn field could become an impenetrable jungle, a hideaway, or an enchanted forest. The hayloft in an old barn could become a pirate ship, a castle, or a frontier fort. An irrigation canal could become a raging river or a lost river of no return. Daydreams are the stuff of writing. "Noveling is the best hobby I've ever had." Mike currently claims fatherhood of three novels: *Thorns of Avarice, Treehouse in the Hood,* and *Clairvoyant.* Find him on Amazon.

STEVE ODENTHAL makes his home in Brigham City and enjoys creating quiet havoc amongst his friends and neighbors. His wife, Valerie, is a creative non-fiction writer and part-time neighborhood peacekeeper. Steve writes plays, screenplays, creative non-fiction, and is currently compiling a collection of "Chimney Fishing" stories about normal things that become humorously abnormal quickly. His work can also be found in Box Elder Magazine where he is a featured humor writer and also in the Utah Humor Anthology, scheduled for publication in 2019. He has been a member of the Brigham City Writers group and The League of Utah Writers for a number of years, and as of yet, neither group has suffered material damages. He is pleased to contribute a few samples of his work to the *Spirals* anthology.

VALERIE ODENTHAL loves dabbling in creative projects. She quests to find delightful adventures including: writing creative non-fiction, children's literature, playwriting, storytelling in Box Elder Magazine, and seeking genres that spark her imagination. When not writing, she can be found creating and designing costumes, props, and sets for Heritage Community Theatre, or building interactive exhibits at the Brigham City Museum of Art & History. Her favorite pastimes include teaching crafts or art, road trips, event planning, and seeking the perfect scone. Valerie is joined by her husband, Steve Odenthal, their five children with their families, and more grandkids than will fit under a blanket fort, as they seek all things fun.

E.B. WHEELER attended BYU, majoring in history with an English minor, and earned graduate degrees in history and landscape architecture from Utah State University. She's the author of seven novels, including Whitney Award finalist *Born to Treason, No Peace with the Dawn, Letters From the Homefront, The Bone Map, and Utah Women: Pioneers, Poets, and Politicians* (forthcoming fall 2019 from The History Press), as well as several short stories, magazine articles, and scripts for educational software programs. The League of Utah Writers named her the 2016 Writer of the Year. In addition to writing, she consults about historic preservation and teaches history at USU.

.

www.ingramcontent.com/pod-product-compliance
Lightning Source LLC
Chambersburg PA
CBHW070935130626

46555CB00001B/439